A SOLDIER LOOKS AT
SPIRITUAL
WARFARE
DICK DENNY

Chosen
Grand Rapids, Michigan

Published by Chosen Books
A division of Baker Publishing Group
P.O. Box 6287, Grand Rapids, MI 49516-6287
www.chosenbooks.com

Printed in the United States of America

Library of Congress Cataloging-in-Publication Data

Denny, Dick, 1923–
    A soldier looks at spiritual warfare / Dick Denny.
        p.   cm.
    ISBN 0-8007-9368-4 (pbk.)
    1. Spiritual warfare. I. Title
    BV4509.5.D46 2004
    235'.4—dc22   2004006564

To God and
my wife, Betty,
who have been my
motivating partners

CONTENTS

ABOUT THIS BOOK

My journey toward God started in 1968, with the death of our oldest son in Vietnam. In 1966 the U.S. government noticed that my son had dropped out of college. His intention was to get married to his fiancée; then both would go to a different school. He received his draft notice during the two months he was out of college. Doing what he thought was right, he went into the Army on his birthday, July 9, 1967.

After basic training at Fort Campbell, Kentucky, he was sent to Camp Polk, Louisiana. He then received a short furlough home, and left for Vietnam on December 13, 1967, from the Twin Cities airport.

That month, my concern for my son started to reveal itself in a dramatic way. I began to dream that he was wounded. The same dream happened seven or eight times within the next month: I could see Rick lying in a foxhole, wounded on his right side and not able to move. In my dream I was crawling to him on my stomach, reaching desperately out to him, but only coming within inches of touching him. Oh, how I struggled; in my dream, I sensed that he was in a life-and-death situation. Being unable to reach him was helpless agony for me.

The last Saturday of January 1968, I went to work at the automotive parts business I owned. After working for a while, I decided to go home early so I could watch my youngest son in a school basketball game.

Shortly after I arrived home, the doorbell rang. My wife had seen the man from Western Union coming up the walk and opened the door to greet him. He had a telegram that she quickly read: "Richard E. Denny Jr. was severely wounded and is not expected to live."

In shock we dashed to the bedroom to pray. We fell on our knees. My wife, Betty, started to pray. All I could do was sob in the confusion of a broken heart. Although I attended Sunday services faithfully and served on church boards, I had not been taught how to pray.

We immediately sent a telegram to our son as he lay dying in a hospital in Vietnam:

> The Spirit of the Lord is around you,
> The prayers of your friends encircle you;
> The hopes of believers surround you;
> The Lord is with you; we are with you.
> There is no distance now!
> You are not alone!

Later we heard through the Red Cross that the telegram was read to each wounded soldier in the field hospital where Rick lay dying. Rick lived only three days after being wounded.

The American Red Cross and the Army confirmed that he had been wounded in the right side by shrapnel. His spinal cord was severed, and he was found in a foxhole just as had been portrayed in my dreams.

The Sunday after Rick's funeral, I promised God that I would follow Christ fully. I sat in the back pew of church, still in the depths of grief and despair. My heart was shattered and broken. It felt like a mountain was crushing me beneath its bulk.

The front of the church bulletin spoke of the apostle Paul's goal, which was expressed to the Philippians: "That I may know him and the power of his resurrection, and may share his sufferings, becoming like him in his death" (Philippians 3:10).

I was reminded that Rick had been concerned about my having a personal relationship with Jesus Christ. He knew that I had recognized a historical Jesus intellectually, but had never surrendered to Christ as my personal Lord and Savior. Although Rick had been brought up going to church, he had committed his life to Christ as a student at St. Olaf College. A singing, witnessing group had come to the college campus and challenged him to acknowledge Christ as his Lord and Savior.

I scratched out Paul's name on the bulletin and inserted Rick's, then passed the bulletin to my wife. She and I had disagreed for years about salvation. She told me that she became a Christian after she struggled into a personal relationship with Christ, after her eighteen-month-old nephew had died from an aneurysm.

My understanding was that salvation came by works. I thought it was up to me to make myself a better person and, at this moment, I sat in despair because I had no hope or understanding of God's grace. A thought suddenly entered my mind—separating, intersecting and cutting across my heaviness and despair. It came almost

11

as a challenge: *It is not what you have done, but what I have done for you.*

Suddenly, new and unheard-of thoughts flooded my mind. The intense heaviness immediately lifted, my mind cleared and suddenly I felt like I was floating in air. It was a powerful spiritual visitation. The Holy Spirit had come in a way I could not deny. For the first time in my life, I experienced the truth that my historical God was *real!*

A new man began emerging from the ashes of the old me. I now knew for certain that salvation was not by good works, but by God's grace. This experience did not mean that I had arrived spiritually, but from that moment I knew that I was headed in the right direction.

As I began to understand spiritual reality, I discovered that Satan, like a jewel thief, had stolen several of my God-given benefits. The enemy had clouded my spiritual eyes, but now I was becoming free. World War II had taught me how to fight against an enemy with physical weapons. Now the Holy Spirit wanted to teach me about spiritual weapons and warfare.

A weapon is anything used to overcome, persuade or get the better of an opponent. An effective soldier knows that each weapon has been made for a specific purpose. He understands its importance and when and where it is to be used. I wanted to become an effective spiritual soldier.

I come from a successful business background, con-firmed by my achievement of the American dream. My business sold products in a five-state upper Midwest area, and I had ten to twenty people working for me. I had time to travel, fly my airplane and enjoy life.

My first conscious spiritual meeting with God changed that life. Encountering God made me hungry and thirsty

12

to explore the spiritual realm. Having now spent more than thirty years in spiritual renewal, I want to share some truths about how to fight spiritual warfare, and how I have learned to live above the negative circumstances of life, by faith and trust in an unchanging God.

I write as a witness to the love of God and share the truths in this book so that you might join me in spiritual warfare. As the blood of Abel was a witness (see Genesis 4:10), my son's blood is also a witness that war is not the true answer to disagreements. The answer is surrender to God.

I want to thank my special Christian friends for helping with this book. It is because of their commitment to God that this book became a reality.

Ron Klug, an editor, challenged me with new ideas, urged me to fill in the blank spots and kept me on target.

Joy McComb, a sister in Christ, made sure that the i's were dotted and the t's crossed.

Thanks to you both.

FOREWORD

As a young man Dick Denny served his country during World War II. He spent five months behind enemy lines after his bomber was shot down over Holland. He learned how to encounter, or to elude, the enemy. He discovered how and when to move safely from place to place. He learned something about warfare, up close and personal.

In midlife Dick and his wife, Betty, were plunged into a different kind of warfare. Their oldest son, Rick, was killed in Vietnam. God came to them in the depth of their grief and kindled their slumbering faith, not only with His comfort but with a call to walk in a new measure of spiritual reality. They soon discovered that along with a greater experience of God's presence came a heightened sense of an enemy presence. They learned something about spiritual warfare, up close and personal.

In this book Dick weaves the two stories together. The lessons he learned as a soldier serve as illustrations or parables of the spiritual warfare he has encountered as a soldier of the Lord Jesus Christ.

One characteristic dominates this book. I can see readers finishing the last chapter, then commenting to a family member or friend, "Hey, this book is practical!"

Take it from Dick Denny, an old soldier who knows what he is talking about: "Spiritual warfare" is not something kooky or spooky. It is reality.

This is a soldier's handbook. It will help you size up the enemy, learn battle and survival skills and ultimately win through to victory.

Larry Christenson

1

PREPARING FOR WAR

The dark clouds of war threatened to engulf Europe in the late 1930s. People had hoped that World War I would be the end to all wars, but now the possibility of a second global conflict was rising like a shadow from the grave.

Hitler believed that Germany should rule Europe and, eventually, the world. His German government had spent years building a large army with powerful tank divisions. Germany's air force was second to none, and they had already taken over several of their smaller neighboring countries.

Italy, led by Benito Mussolini, had also built a large army and air force. He sided with Germany, and together they began to form the power known as "The Axis." In the Far East, Japan's army and navy were expanding.

England, France and Russia felt threatened by the Axis countries. They, too, had built up their forces and were getting ready to face Germany and Italy in a conflict. Almost every country in Europe started to expand and build its armed services. Even the United States responded to what was happening in Europe by drafting men to build up a so-called peacetime army.

Then on December 7, 1941, the Japanese attacked the U.S. Naval base at Pearl Harbor, Hawaii. The American government declared war on Japan and Germany, and countless young men saw the need to defend our way of life against the enemy's aggression.

I answered the Axis' challenge in 1943 by enlisting in the Army Air Corps (which was to become the Air Force). Leaving a small Indian village in northern Minnesota and going off to war was a major step in my nineteen-year-old life. My parents took me to the station in Bemidji, where I caught my train to the induction center at Fort Snelling in St. Paul. I shook my father's hand as a real man would do. Then I shook my mother's hand. I can still see the tears that sprang to her eyes when I did not hug her good-bye. I knew she wanted to hug the son whom she had loved for nineteen years, but I was too "grown up." I still pay the price for being macho: My mother died three months later at the age of 46.

World War II was now a big part of the Denny family. Never once did I question where I would be sent, because I was willing to die for what I believed was right. I knew that I needed training for the call that I felt so strongly—the call to fight for my country.

My training taught me how to march in unison with others, so that we could function as a team. As soldiers we learned to protect our brothers against any enemy.

After learning discipline and care for others, I was trained to do every possible mechanical fix that a B-17 could need when it was in flight. Then I was sent to a Las Vegas gunnery school where I learned about 50-caliber machine guns and the dynamics that come into play when shooting—whether from a moving truck, an airplane or a standstill. From there I went on to Rapid City, South Dakota, to train as part of a ten-man bomber crew. Our training was a learning experience conducted in a protected environment, and it had one focus: preparation for actual combat with the enemy.

Knowing the Enemy

In World War II, the primary enemies of freedom were the three countries of Germany, Italy and Japan. As a soldier in the Air Force I knew the enemy's identity. It was part of my job. It was much later that I discovered that Christians have an enemy who desires to spiritually annihilate us. His weapons of warfare are different from the weapons of World War II. The weapons of Satan are deceit, distortion and disunity.

The apostle Paul writes, "For though we live in the world we are not carrying on a worldly war, for the weapons of our warfare are not worldly but have divine power to destroy strongholds" (2 Corinthians 10:3–4).

Our spiritual weapons are supplied from God's vast arsenal. The Holy Spirit has given us God's Word and authority over Satan. His work in our lives produces love, forgiveness and effective prayer. These, and many others, are the gifts that will help every Christian win in spiritual warfare.

When I came to the knowledge that there is a battle between Satan and God almighty, I chose to align myself with the winning side. For the second time in my life, I made a decision to serve and fight for what I believe.

Jesus is quoted in the book of Matthew: "No one can serve two masters; for either he will hate the one and love the other, or he will be devoted to the one and despise the other. You cannot serve God and mammon" (Matthew 6:24). We choose whom we want to serve.

I was taught during my first years in church that Christians have three enemies: the world, the flesh and the devil. I have a simpler view that is based on the laws of combat. I believe that an enemy is anyone, or anything, that keeps us from doing God's will. It just so happens that nearly all of our enemies fall into one of those three categories. We will be discussing the devil as our enemy extensively. I want to mention a brief word about the world and the flesh.

As I struggled with how to define what the Bible calls "the world," I came to the conclusion that the philosophies of our world form an evil system that opposes God. They do not value the same things God does. They do not lead us in submission to Him, and anything that is not of God's will, plan and purpose is evil.

Whether these philosophies are perpetuated by governments, business, entertainment or economic systems, they represent "the world." Many people use them as guidelines for their lives, but worldly philosophies cannot save us for eternal life. They only make our lifelong journey more dangerous and difficult.

The apostle Paul writes to the Colossians, "See to it that no one makes a prey of you by philosophy and empty deceit, according to human tradition, according to the elemental spirits of the universe, and not according to Christ" (Colossians 2:8).

I found that worldly philosophies are a dangerous spiritual foundation. They were designed that way on purpose; each one developed under Satan's deceitful influence. Ever so subtly, they encourage us to trust in money, power and ourselves—in everything but God. Businesses, marriages and lives crumble endlessly, as people frantically wedge new supports into their foundations. As the weight of life builds, their supports collapse and Satan finds them crippled prey.

Defining the enemy called "flesh" is easy. I am constantly aware that there is a part of me that wants to go its own way. It motivates me to be self-serving. When I feel proud or self-satisfied, it is because my flesh has been in action, working in rebellion against the will and plan of God.

Jonah is a classic example of a man with his flesh in action. God asked Jonah to go and preach repentance to the city of Nineveh. Jonah thought he had a better idea than God and fled to Tarshish instead. His flesh (or self-centered old nature) did not *want* to preach repentance to the heathen city! The Ninevites were age-old enemies of Israel, and Jonah rather liked the idea of them dying under God's judgment (see Jonah 1:1–3).

You probably know the story: God had Jonah nearly shipwrecked, swallowed by a fish and spit out on a beach three days later. At that point Jonah was happy to preach to Nineveh. The Lord would not allow His servant to be a deserter. Jonah's flesh had to submit to God's plan, and our flesh is no different. If our flesh is not put to death, we cannot win in spiritual warfare.

21

Knowing My Commander

Enlisting with God meant that I would need to undergo the training of the Holy Spirit. His school is where we learn how to function in the unseen spiritual world and to have the mind of Christ, so that our thinking reflects the will of God. We are taught how to walk in faith and to discern the different spirits we encounter and about the many other weapons and facets of the spiritual world.

In 1968 the Holy Spirit broke through to my unspiritual heart by the death of my son Rick in Vietnam. I wanted and needed something different. My old way of living the American dream was no longer sufficient. That is when I began my Holy Spirit training for a deeper understanding of life, its purpose and how I fit into God's scheme for life. The Holy Spirit began to take me on a journey, showing me the difference between walking in my self-centered old nature and walking with Him.

According to Scripture my heart was not right before God. I had to stop thinking about God serving me and start thinking about me serving God. Instead of trying to fit God into my life, I became more interested in who He was and how I fit into His life. I was in the process of learning what it means to be a Christian who is spiritually alive.

I grew up attending church and had been taught that baptism was the pinnacle of my spiritual life. Being baptized and attending church on Sunday was all that God could require of anyone. I did not know there was more to the Christian life than what I was experiencing. As my wife has said, "We have never been opposed to God; we were just ignorant of Him and our enemy."

The Air Force prepared me for aerial combat. Now the Holy Spirit was preparing me for spiritual combat by awakening me to a personal relationship with the Lord!

I had not understood that God wanted a personal relationship with me. The apostle Paul writes to the Corinthians, "God is faithful, by whom you were called into the fellowship of his Son, Jesus Christ our Lord" (1 Corinthians 1:9).

I had an intellectual recognition of a historical Christ who lived two thousand years ago, but Satan had prevented me from desiring a spiritual *relationship*. I needed to receive the truth of God's desire for me: fellowship with Him through His Son, Jesus Christ.

My wife has said, "The depth of a relationship is measured by the extent we are willing to work at it." The same truth applies to a relationship with God. I had not worked at my relationship because of my ignorance.

My friend Pastor Don Potenhauer put it precisely: "Walking with the Lord is like playing a game of checkers. He moves, then it is our move. If we do not move, the game stops right there."

I wanted to move! I found that I was called to serve God without any reservations or preconceived ideas about how His army should be managed. God's army does not march to the cadence of opinions, but rather to the commands of its Triune leadership: Father, Son and Holy Spirit. God wanted me to learn about Him as my spiritual Commander-in-Chief.

In all warfare it is essential to know that we have leadership we can trust. I needed to learn to trust my Commander. If I did not know the strengths of my Commander-in-Chief, I would never realize the resources available to me as His soldier. Previously I had known *about* God, but now the Holy Spirit wanted me to know *Him*. He began by teaching me three of God's main characteristics: His presence, His knowledge and His power. Understanding these facets is fundamental to spiritual warfare.

When I encountered God for the first time, my awareness and commitment to Him changed. I discovered I could not go to the bathroom without Him. He would not stay outside the door. God became that close!

Yes, I could shut Him out of my life by ignoring Him. I could choose to exclude Him from my decisions and activities, but that could not change the fact that He is always near. I found that the slightest awareness of Him on my part brought His acknowledgment of me. Whether I was in a time of troubled darkness or a moment of extreme joy, I could not leave God outside my life. I was like a goldfish in a bowl of water, unable to escape His presence.

God has total knowledge of everything past, present and future. It was important for me to discover this truth. My self-centered old nature had a tendency to compromise. Sinning was a little easier, from the worldly point of view, if I thought no one else knew. Once I encountered God's manifest presence, I soon learned that my conscience and God *both* knew when I tried to deny a conviction of sin. My guilty conscience became touchy and allowed me no sleep if I was in the wrong.

The psalmist writes, "Thou knowest when I sit down and when I rise up; thou discernest my thoughts from afar. Thou searchest out my path and my lying down, and art acquainted with all my ways. Even before a word is on my tongue, lo, O LORD, thou knowest it altogether" (Psalm 139:2–4).

I have found that God has universal and unlimited power over His creation. I have been engaged in spiritual warfare where the knowledge of God's sovereignty was the only thing that kept me going. I know that He has the final word in whatever happens in my life. Because of that knowledge, I can trust Him.

At His trial before Pontius Pilate, Jesus said, "You would have no power over me unless it had been given you from above . . ." (John 19:11). There is only One who has the final authority in spiritual warfare—God!

Once I began to understand these characteristics of God's nature, the Holy Spirit began to prepare me for my next lesson. He had revealed to me what my Commander was like, and now He wanted to show me what *I* was like as a spiritual soldier.

Knowing Myself

The Air Force prepared me for a physical war, but not a spiritual war. The Holy Spirit wanted to teach me about my basic makeup and why I function the way I do.

I began to discover that my life was led by my soul—the self-centered old nature also called the "flesh." What my conscious mind and will decided, my body followed, and my spirit tagged along behind. It was backward, like the tail wagging the dog!

The Holy Spirit told me that my self-centered way of thinking needed to change. By giving me new thoughts, God was challenging the way I went about life. I found that letting my spirit lead all week, and not just on Sunday, caused spiritual warfare!

My mind had been programmed from childhood for worldly thinking seven days a week. My soul, relying on the five senses of touch, taste, vision, hearing and smell, did not want to submit to the Holy Spirit. God wanted my spirit to be led by His. The enemy wanted my soul to lead. Spiritual warfare began when I demanded that my soul give up command of my decisions. Consequently my mind became the battlefield between good and evil.

The process of changing leadership from soul to spirit is called *sanctification*. It is the process of taking our world-oriented thinking and replacing it with spiritual thoughts and eternal consciousness. This is why it is so important to understand how the Holy Spirit, our spirit and our soul function together. This way the tactics of the enemy can be understood and dealt with in spiritual warfare.

Knowing My Soul

I believe that the soul is composed of three faculties: mind, will and emotions. The mind has the capacity to comprehend ideas, but not the ability to execute. It has the power to think and reason. The will is the mental faculty by which one deliberately chooses or decides upon a course of action. The will and mind work together to accomplish what they agree upon. The emotions are the mental condition marked by excitement or stimulation of the passions or sensibilities. Emotions are not meant to lead, but to express and confirm the decisions of the mind and will.

When the Holy Spirit leads, then the soul follows in its proper sequence, joined to our body. It is like a river flowing through three connected lakes. The river starts with the Holy Spirit, connects with our spirit, and goes through to our soul. Then what is decided upon is acted out through the physical body (see John 7:37–39).

Our body is the container for the spirit and soul. The apostle Paul writes, "But we have this treasure in earthen vessels, to show that the transcendent power belongs to God and not to us" (2 Corinthians 4:7).

Knowing My Spirit

The spirit also has three facets: intuition, conscience and communion. *Intuition* is the faculty of our spirit through which we know truth without conscious reasoning, almost as if by instinct. To perceive truth without human comprehension or understanding is a spiritual power. It can be nothing else, because our fallen nature wars with God—it does not instinctively turn to His truth.

Life—the Christian life in particular—brings us many difficult situations. These problems are often strategic situations in which the Holy Spirit reveals to us God's knowledge and wisdom. These are times when we "just know"—and we are certain. We know that we know.

Our *conscience* is the faculty that reveals the difference between right and wrong. This God-given tool is a delicate one and can, to a certain extent, be misused. Some people override their conscience by justifying themselves until the simple question of right and wrong becomes cloudy. When this happens, the conscience can become dull from many deliberately repeated wrong choices. That is why it needs to be continually shaped and sharpened to reflect God's values and Word.

A conscience that is spiritually alive understands that it must convict us according to the high law of righteousness, but accept God's forgiveness and grace when we repent. A conscience that can find the balance between law and grace helps us to live confidently in the freedom of God's love!

Communion is the bridge that connects our spirit with the Holy Spirit. It is the ability to actually relate to God, and it is a miracle. We, created out of matter, can have relationship with the infinite Spirit of our Creator!

In my preparation for spiritual warfare, I first had to learn to know my enemies, know my new Commander and know myself. Then I was ready to learn about spiritual warfare. This book is a manual for basic training in spiritual warfare. It is based on the lessons I learned over many years as a spiritual soldier. In the coming chapters you will learn:

- How the Holy Spirit empowers us for transformation and dynamic life changes in the process of spiritual warfare
- The importance of God's authority in spiritual warfare
- How Satan attacks our minds and how we can defend ourselves
- How to protect ourselves through joy, peace and self-control
- The key role of faith in spiritual warfare
- The importance of prayer—our method of communication on the spiritual battlefield
- A better understanding of Satan's battlefield tactics

- How Satan targets God, individuals, families and friends
- How forgiveness can help us reclaim territory lost to Satan
- How to face suffering on the spiritual battlefield
- How to fight back through spiritual ministry

2

FIREPOWER

The Holy Spirit in Action

One of my favorite training experiences was at the Air Force school in Las Vegas. There I learned how to fire a 12-gauge shotgun from a moving vehicle. To train for this, I stood in the back of a pickup truck as the driver bumped over the desert terrain. As we went, I would suddenly be confronted with a flying clay pigeon (a round disc about six inches in diameter, made of clay and shaped like a Frisbee). The disk was shot into the air from a concealed place. I never knew where this clay pigeon would come from, so I constantly scanned a 360-degree circle. This was to help me be alert for a future enemy attack from any direction.

I watched many films with simulated attacks by German fighters. Once I was in Europe, when the German fighter planes attacked with their weapons firing, it was like watching a training film. My training had taught me to be vigilant.

Standing in a moving vehicle helped me learn balance. I also learned how to lead and hit a moving target. The training was necessary because I was going to be confronted by an enemy in a moving airplane who wanted to kill me. As I advanced in gunnery training, I was assigned to ride in the back cockpit of an airplane with a 50-caliber gun. A second plane, towing a large canvas bull's-eye, would fly alongside. My challenge was to shoot the bull's-eye.

When I finished shooting, I wiggled my gun to show that I was through, and my pilot would pull away from the target. As we pulled away, I felt like I was going through the bottom of the airplane. What pressure! I loved it!

At other times we would fly low and shoot at stationary targets on the ground. I was learning the dynamics of correlating the speed of the airplane with distance in order to hit moving or sitting targets.

When I started shooting 50-caliber machine guns, I saw what firepower could do. As the projectiles tore through my targets, I experienced power. Seeing the results of the destruction made me aware of my responsibility for this power.

Spiritual Firepower

Not long ago we went through an electrical power outage at home. This made life more difficult because most things require electricity. If power was not available on a regular basis, we would have to make an adjustment for the lack of power. We would live at a lower level of lifestyle.

The world runs on power. Many people spend their lives seeking power by stepping on and climbing over others on the way to the top. Worldly power has people fighting to get it. If you have power, others are subject to you. If you do not, you are subject to those in power.

The power in human warfare goes to the one who has the best strategy, resources and sophisticated weaponry. Spiritual power is different. Spiritual power is simply received and released. Whereas military power is always destructive, God's power is always released for good. God never asks us to do anything unless He supplies the power. He will not give us His spiritual power unless we ask what He wants us to do!

After Rick's death I recommitted my life to Christ. Within a year after my recommitment, I began to go back to my old ways of being a Christian. I knew that I needed spiritual power in my life, but I had no idea of what I should do.

My wife, Betty, attended a Bible study conducted by a new friend, Pat Ose. One evening Betty invited Pat and her husband, Glenn, to come over for pie and coffee. I happened to look out the picture window and noticed they were walking up the driveway carrying big, black Bibles.

I asked my wife, "What are Lutherans doing with Bibles?" None of the Lutherans I knew at that time carried Bibles anywhere!

They came into the house and within fifteen minutes were praying for my wife with the laying on of hands, asking God to baptize her with the Holy Spirit. Betty, who was normally quiet and reserved, began speaking with authority in a strange language. She had been filled with Holy Spirit power!

Pat and Glenn asked me if I would like prayer, but at that time I was not hungering or thirsting for more of God. I wanted my wife to change, but I was not ready to grow spiritually. I still found comfort in my powerless but familiar Christian lifestyle.

I was like the man driving from Minnesota to Florida, puttering along lost in thought. Suddenly he saw flashing red lights on a police car alongside. Coming out of his daze, he saw the police officer motioning him to pull over to the side of the road and obeyed immediately. He was now wide awake. When the officer came beside his car, the man rolled down his window.

The officer spoke, "Sir, your taillights and brake lights are not working." The man paused for a moment, then suddenly slammed his door open and raced to the back of his car, sending the officer sprawling to the pavement. Before even reaching the back of the car, he screamed, "Oh, no! Oh, no!" Tears ran down his cheeks as he wept loudly.

The officer regrouped with great patience and approached the man sympathetically. "I am just stopping you because your taillights and brake lights are not working. Why all the fuss?"

The man cried out with great anxiety, "Where is my trailer, with my wife and three kids?"

Like this man, I had settled into a "comfort zone," taking God, family and friends for granted. I had been lulled to sleep by the enemy. My Christian walk was that of a sleepwalker, not an overcoming soldier. God wanted me out of the comfort zone to learn how to fight spiritual warfare.

As the months went by, I witnessed the Holy Spirit do a transforming work in my wife. Life for her had been very difficult because of the death of our son in Vietnam. With the baptism in the Holy Spirit she became less introspective, more outgoing and at peace with herself. She read the Scriptures with enthusiasm and received understanding of what the Holy Spirit had written.

For several months I watched her change. Seeing the change in her brought me to a point where I desired the same spiritual energy. I began to hunger and thirst for more of God. I, too, wanted to be filled with Holy Spirit power. As Matthew writes, "Blessed are those who hunger and thirst for righteousness, for they shall be satisfied" (Matthew 5:6).

Filled with Holy Spirit Power

At my request, Pastor Fred Herzog, a Spirit-filled Covenant pastor whom I had met earlier, came to my home one Monday morning. Fred, Betty and I sat at the kitchen table. He began to unfold the scriptural basis for the "baptism of the Holy Spirit."

John the Baptist said, "I baptize you with water for repentance, but he who is coming after me is mightier than I, whose sandals I am not worthy to carry; he will baptize you with the Holy Spirit and with fire" (Matthew 3:11). John was speaking of Jesus and His baptism by the Holy Spirit.

Jesus was baptized in the Jordan river, and the Spirit of God descended from heaven as a dove alighting on Him. Matthew describes what happened when Jesus was baptized: "A voice [came] from heaven, saying 'This is my beloved Son, with whom I am well pleased'" (Matthew 3:17).

Then Fred told about healings, casting out of demons and the ministry Jesus' disciples had before Pentecost. Jesus had sent seventy disciples out into the villages of Israel. They later returned with joy and excitement in their hearts, exclaiming, "Lord, even the demons are subject to us in your name!" (Luke 10:17).

And Jesus said to them, "I saw Satan fall like lightning from heaven. Behold, I have given you authority to tread upon serpents and scorpions, and over all the power of the enemy; and nothing shall hurt you" (Luke 10:17–19).

Fred told us how fearful the disciples were after the crucifixion. The Lord appeared to them in a locked room and said,

> "Peace be with you. As the Father has sent me, even so I send you." And when he had said this, he breathed on them, and said to them, "Receive the Holy Spirit. If you forgive the sins of any, they are forgiven; if you retain the sins of any, they are retained."
>
> John 20:21–23

Later Jesus said, "And behold, I send the promise of my Father upon you; but stay in the city, until you are clothed with power from on high" (Luke 24:49).

Jesus was talking about the promise made by the prophet Joel centuries earlier. Joel had prophesied:

> "And it shall come to pass afterward, that I will pour out my spirit on all flesh; your sons and your daughters shall prophesy, your old men shall dream dreams, and your young men shall see visions. Even upon the menservants and maidservants in those days, I will pour out my spirit."
>
> Joel 2:28–29

Fred told me that just before Jesus ascended He said, "But you shall receive power when the Holy Spirit has come upon you; and you shall be my witnesses in Jerusalem and in all Judea and Samaria and to the end of the earth" (Acts 1:8).

In Greek this power is called *dunamis*, from which we get our word *dynamite*. It is a spiritual explosive power released to bring change.

Fred explained that 120 people, men and women in the Upper Room, were praying and seeking God's will. When their self-centered old natures had quieted down, they were ready to hear God speak. A sound came from heaven like the rush of a mighty wind filling the place where they were sitting. There appeared to them tongues as of fire, and they were all filled with the Holy Spirit.

There were many Jews near the place where the 120 were meeting. At the sound of the Holy Spirit's visitation, they realized that something was happening and began to gather. They were amazed by the sound and the sight of the 120, praising God in dozens of languages. Some mocked and said, "They are filled with new wine," implying that the 120 were drunk. Satan has his critics at every spiritual party.

Then Peter stood up and gave the Jews a history lesson. Speaking with authority, he told the mockers that they were seeing the fulfillment of the promise given to the prophet Joel. He finished by saying that they were guilty of crucifying the Messiah! Peter's words cut to their hearts and they asked, "Brethren, what shall we do?"

Peter responded:

"Repent, and be baptized every one of you in the name of Jesus Christ for the forgiveness of your sins; and you shall receive the gift of the Holy Spirit. For the promise

37

is to you and to your children and to all that are far off, every one whom the Lord our God calls to him."

Acts 2:38–39

That satisfied me. When Fred said that, I heard my invitation to be baptized in the Holy Spirit. I was ready to receive the spiritual power God had for me, just as the 120 experienced in the Upper Room. I did not have to wait, I just needed to ask and receive. I was now ready to move beyond my comfort zone into the unknown.

As Fred laid his hands on me and prayed, I experienced a strange feeling of being satisfied, like after a good home-cooked meal. I broke out sobbing, which lasted about thirty seconds, then stopped as fast as it started. Waves of peace flooded my entire being.

My life has not been the same since. I received a hunger and thirst to know more about the unseen spiritual world where eventually I will live forever. I had heard about charismatics, but now I was one. God was preparing me for spiritual warfare.

Life-Changing Power for All

My Air Force training had showed me what the powerful 50-caliber machine guns could do. Now Jesus wanted me to experience the power of the Holy Spirit. Just as the Air Force taught me responsibility with guns and bombs, the Holy Spirit wanted to teach me to flow in His power. Taking the step of faith to be baptized in the Holy Spirit moved me into a new spiritual realm.

What is the Lord's basic will for all Christians? The apostle Paul writes, "Therefore do not be foolish, but understand what the will of the Lord is. And do not get drunk with wine, for that is debauchery; but be filled with the Spirit" (Ephesians 5:17–18). *Being filled with Holy Spirit power* means being in the center of God's will.

Out of this initial receiving of spiritual power burst a desire. My heart was called to a different lifestyle; one of being involved in God's plan and purpose, which included spiritual warfare. When we have been touched by the Holy Spirit, life cannot be the same!

Fred told me that for most of history the Holy Spirit had visited earth to do God's will and then left. With the outpouring described in Acts 2, the Spirit now came to stay, living in human hearts. The Spirit of truth had come to convict me of sin, guide me into all truth and declare the things that are to come. Now my life could glorify God, because the power was here to reveal His life. I experienced a hunger and thirst for God's Word, along with a new understanding of life.

Fred went on to share that *charisma* means "God's grace, favor and kindness." God reveals spiritual gifts when the receiver is willing to yield to and depend on the Holy Spirit. The *gifts* of the Holy Spirit are cultivating tools to help produce the *fruit* of the Spirit. Fred said, "The spiritual gifts are not something we do, but what the Holy Spirit does through us. The gifts and fruit of the Spirit should be a normal, natural and supernatural way of life for all Christians. Because we lack teaching on this subject, many people quench the gifts of the Spirit and live a powerless life. God wants all His people open to the spiritual gifts and producing fruit to build up the body of believers."

I discovered later that charismatic Christians often have trouble fitting into a typical church congregation. They act differently from the preconceived ideas of how a Christian should act. They become God's instrument to bring conviction, a message that the Church has settled for less than what God has to offer.

It is not easy to allow Jesus to be Lord of our lives unless we are spending time with Him through His Word, prayer, fellowship and Bible study. As the lordship of Jesus Christ becomes more complete in our lives, some people will draw back, as did some of the disciples (see John 6:66–69).

Some will follow Him from a distance. Others will forge ahead focused on God and His plan and realizing that there is no other way for them. I did not want to follow at a distance anymore. I wanted to walk with God, and I soon determined that there was no room for my worldly clutter. God's Pentecostal power was given to overcome the spiritual traditionalism in my life.

Soon after my experience a pastor asked me, "Which of the three main church festivals do you appreciate the most: Christmas, Easter or Pentecost?"

I replied, "All three are important as they flow together. If there was no Christmas, neither Easter nor Pentecost could mean anything, and the opposite is true." My next comment was, "Pentecost."

Both Christmas and Easter are commemorative: Christ need not experience another birth, death or resurrection. That was accomplished once and for all time. When Christ said from the cross, "It is finished," His call and the work our Father had given Him were complete (see John 19:30). The powers of darkness had been defeated. Now all things were put in subjection to Christ, and He is forever seated at the right hand of God.

Pentecost was not meant to be commemorative! Pentecost is an ongoing work of the Holy Spirit. There is no benediction at the end of the book of Acts. This book is still being written by the Church today. When the Holy Spirit was given at Pentecost, His work was not completed but entered a new phase. The Holy Spirit desires to move today, just as freely as when those 120 people experienced an outpouring of His Pentecostal power in the Upper Room.

I discovered that a personal Pentecost is God breaking into this time-space world. His desire is to release His power to those who have open hearts and ears. Our desire should be to receive the Holy Spirit's power to live as overcomers and become Spirit-filled witnesses. If the millions who take the name "Christian" were to be filled with the Holy Spirit and applied the Scriptures to their lives, this world would be turned rightside up.

At a meeting, several pastors were discussing what they were going to do at their upcoming Sunday Pentecost service. After some discussion I said, "What will happen is that most Lutheran pastors will give a history lesson about Pentecost from the pulpit, and their congregations will go home." I was not being sarcastic but acknowledging that church members should have more than a history lesson as incentive to gather on Pentecost morning.

I went on to say, "Just imagine if on Sunday morning all Christians were willing to receive the baptism of the Holy Spirit. As the pastor led us in prayer we would pray in agreement, 'Yes, Father, I desire to be filled anew with the Holy Spirit. Cleanse me from anything that stands between us. I yield to You that Your power might flow in and through me. In all aspects of my life I desire to become Christ-conscious and let the Holy Spirit lead and guide me. Please baptize me in the Holy Spirit.'"

Everyone who has come into the Church through the new birth needs power to grow spiritually. Many have salvation but lack spiritual power to understand the call to sanctification, witnessing and spiritual warfare. Without Holy Spirit power, we cannot live the life of Pentecost or fight spiritual warfare.

This spiritual power is released in a dynamic way to help grace and faith bring a deep hunger for spiritual growth and fulfillment in life. Many Christians have found that the *way* to eternal life is the cross, the *truth* reveals the potential of abundant life, but spiritual *life* is lived in the power of the Holy Spirit!

Power to Change

God's power is always given for a reason. I had received His power. Now what would be my next step? What did He want to change? I soon became aware that He wanted to change *me*!

For much of my life I was naively cohabitating with the enemy. Even though I was a Christian, the enemy was subtly controlling me. The Holy Spirit wanted me to learn how to break that satanic bondage. He wanted me free in Christ!

When I was a child in northern Minnesota, the Civilian Conservation Corps burned off land as a management technique. After the fire, new life would spring forth. Many of the prairie flowers would bloom only if there had been a fire the year before. New life was possible, but it required the old life to die.

I needed to learn how to yield to the power of the Holy Spirit. I had preconceived ideas of what it meant to be a Christian, but they were wrong. I soon found that new spiritual life flows out of the death of my self-centered old nature. I needed the dross of sin burnt off so Holy Spirit power for the new life could be brought forth. How could this happen?

The apostle Paul writes:

> For those who live according to the flesh set their minds on the things of the flesh, but those who live according to the Spirit set their minds on the things of the Spirit. To set the mind on the flesh is death, but to set the mind on the Spirit is life and peace.
>
> Romans 8:5–6

I soon found out that the Bible reveals two kinds of death: the physical death and, as we learn how to walk with God, the death of our self-centered old nature. An old evangelist described the physical death as simply shedding what was dead anyway.

1. *Physical death requires the grace of God and the fullness of His time.* The writer of Hebrews says, "And just as it is appointed for men to die once, and after that comes judgment . . ." (Hebrews 9:27). Death is a reminder of our mortality and that our time on earth is limited.

When Christ died, He found that physical death had no power over Him. Whoever believes in Christ shares the same truth—that the sting of death has been taken away. We may go about life, living in the fullness of faith, for we know our final destination!

In physical death we have no choice but to surrender the power of our wills to our Creator. I believe that no one dies ahead of or behind God's appointed time. We may not understand the timing of a loved one's death, but it is always an opportunity for the survivors to draw closer to God.

43

2. *The second death deals with our self-centered old nature, also known as the flesh.* When we are born anew into the spiritual realm, we receive a new nature. Spiritual warfare begins immediately between the new nature led by God and the self-centered old nature influenced by Satan.

The alternative to our old nature is our new spiritual nature. The new nature will flourish if, by an act of our wills, the self-centered old nature is put to death on the cross. If we choose to revert to the deeds of the self-centered old nature, our new nature will starve to death.

Death to our self-centered old nature will cause difficult struggles in our minds. It calls for discerning and choosing between the leading of the Holy Spirit and the desires of our self-centered old nature. The result is spiritual warfare!

Paul writes to the Romans, "For if you live according to the flesh [self-centered old nature] you will die, but if by the Spirit you put to death the deeds of the body you will live" (Romans 8:13). To put to death the deeds of our body means that the will of God comes first in our lives. His will is chosen over our desire to be first in our thought patterns.

What is our fleshly, self-centered old nature like? Paul writes to the Galatians: "Now the works of the flesh are plain: fornication, impurity, licentiousness, idolatry, sorcery, enmity, strife, jealousy, anger, selfishness, dissension, party spirit, envy, drunkenness, carousing, and the like . . ." (Galatians 5:19–20). That is a formidable list, but a good reason why we need spiritual power to put to death our self-centered old nature.

My self-centered old nature is tough. About the time I think he is away for good, he shows up, poking his ugly head into things and trying to take over as he always has in the past.

My self-centered old nature has an insidious, subtle way of coming to the surface in the midst of relationships. He will say, "I am not to blame," and refuse to be humbled. He is unteachable when he gets like this and not open to reason, because he is "always right."

He wants to be involved in everything, and he never has God's best interest at heart. At one time in my life I had thought that he had gone away. Finished! I was so happy. But as soon as I began to interact with other people, he showed up again and wanted to do things his way.

My flesh is so great at interrupting people that he should win a first-place medal. (He would like that a lot, by the way.) He always wants the last word; always seems to have a better idea of how things should work. Sometimes he wants to yell, especially if his children irritate him.

If I let him, this petty tyrant will take over my life. I used to think that he might change some day. No way—it is not on his agenda. He is very defensive at times, and to listen to him you would think that he graduated from Harvard Law School with top honors.

Many times he has said something that he should not have said. Last week he really gave me a bad time when he got angry at a friend. He would not shut up and let my friend talk. Do you think he would apologize? No, he remained adamant that he was right. Now I do not anticipate seeing that friend again very soon.

With his self-righteous, unforgiving attitude, my self-centered old nature refused to listen. He maintained that it is better to be self-righteous and right than to admit he was wrong. I asked him, *Which is more important, to be right or loving?* He snapped back at me and said, *Right.*

After that he would not let me get in a word. It sure is difficult to carry on a conversation with someone who is always right.

When he seems to be wrong, he protects himself by dredging something up from the past. It is always something where he can point to being "right."

He mentioned that someone had cut in front of him on the freeway. He said, *Something snapped within me and encouraged me to pay that driver back and give him a little extra.* He mentioned the different thoughts that went through his mind, even running the other driver off the road.

He does not understand forgiveness at all, as his attitude is, *I always get even.* He does not comprehend how his attitude can poison my spiritual system, just as a rattlesnake bite would send poison throughout my body.

Someone from church told me that we are actors on the stage of life, with only three in the audience: Father, Son and Holy Spirit. My self-centered old nature really was unhappy to hear that, because he felt as though he had the right to voice his opinion if on a Sunday morning the pastor or song leader did not do it his way.

He said, *After all, I do come here every week. What's wrong with expecting a perfect service? Is God not perfect? I am positive He expects a perfect service as I do.* (He believes that his idea of what is "right" should be everyone's standard.)

After he quieted down, he let me speak. I said, *Buster, you have given me considerable trouble for years. I have had it with you. I have been listening to your grumbling and I will admit you do not grumble like you used to, but I'll tell you what I am going to do. I thought one funeral was enough, but you seem to need another. I am going to your funeral whenever I cry "Abba, Father," for it is the Holy Spirit Himself bearing witness that you are dead! I am going to reckon my self-centered old nature dead to sin and alive to God in Christ Jesus!* (see Romans 6:11).

What I have been describing is the self-centered old nature in action. The old nature with its desire to be king is subtly led by pride against the new nature. This self-centered old nature gave the apostle Paul a lot of problems until he learned where and how this new nature fit into the whole scheme of life. With his self-centered old nature, Paul served the law of sin and death. But he discovered that he could serve the new nature and God's laws with both his heart and his mind, if he was led by the Holy Spirit.

What constitutes the new nature? The new nature revealed is love, joy, peace, patience, kindness, goodness, faithfulness, gentleness and self-control (see Galatians 5:22). The new nature loves forgiveness, justice and mercy, and counts others better than self. Whatever encourages and channels God's love to another person is the new nature in action.

Being led by the spirit or by the soul determines our destiny, as the following diagram indicates.

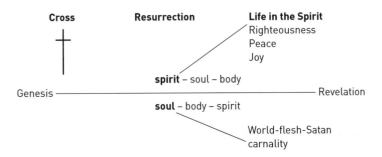

The cross is where my sinful *will* crosses the *will* of God.

47

The Will to Power

How is the privilege of choice best exercised? Where will the power come from if I make the choice of putting to death the deeds of the fleshly self-centered old nature?

Power is supplied by the one we choose to obey: God or Satan. This is why it is so important to understand how the will enters the picture to put to death the deeds of the flesh. The choice of our will causes spiritual warfare!

There is only one place God wants our self-centered old nature to go—to the cross! The Holy Spirit will not take our self-centered old nature to the cross; we do so by choosing God's will rather than ours. The Spirit will not do what He has given us permission and power to do. He will set up circumstances and supply the power for us to take our self-centered old nature to the cross. As we put it to death by an act of our will, the new nature has freedom to do God's will. The cross is the best place for the self-centered old nature.

Whenever I get into a situation where I need to put my self-centered old nature to death, I picture the cross in my mind. At those times, the cross is the safest place for me. On the cross I find freedom from having to be right, freedom to love others who stand in opposition and freedom to be what God created me to be. I can only be spiritually free when my self-centered old nature is on the cross!

My family, tired and exhausted, was coming back late Sunday evening from a weekend at our cabin. We had been water-skiing along with the usual family activities. I was singing worship songs over in my mind—songs of renewal.

About seven miles from the cabin my wife suddenly exclaimed, "I left all the swimming suits on the clothesline! We will not be back for another week. We have to get them!" This meant fourteen extra miles at 10:00 at night.

I was facing a decision of who would control: the self-centered old nature (who wanted to be sour) or my new nature. Singing the renewal songs had prepared my mind to obey the new nature. I continued singing, turned around in the next driveway and went back to the cabin. I had power to overcome the enemy, because I chose God's way. Satan lost that battle in spiritual warfare.

Paul must have experienced some family outings, because he said it this way: "For while we live we are always being given up to death for Jesus' sake, so that the life of Jesus may be manifested in our mortal flesh. So death is at work in us, but life in you" (2 Corinthians 4:11–12). The indwelling presence of the Spirit in believers is a pledge by God that He will quicken our spirits and show us how and when to put to death the deeds of the body.

Anything that stands in opposition to God needs to be put to death on the cross by an act of our will. At the cross is where our will intersects the will of God. Each time we choose to put to death the deeds of our flesh by an act of our will, we give others an opportunity to experience God's life and love. God's power brings us into spiritual maturity and freedom!

When we allow Holy Spirit power to fill us, our lifestyles will testify to the death of our self-centered old nature. When Holy Spirit power is released it takes us to the cross, where we overcome the enemy. At the cross we begin to learn what it is to be led by God's powerful spiritual authority!

3

LEARNING SPIRITUAL AUTHORITY

Learning about authority in the Air Force was no problem for me. I had a father who was a strict disciplinarian, and I learned about the lines of authority at an early age. Because of this, I have always had respect for people in positions of authority. If I was questioned by my father about my behavior concerning school or any other area where we disagreed, I had to prove why I was right. I was guilty until proven innocent. But I was happy and free to be under authority because my father was responsible in taking care of me, as were the officers I later served under in the Air Force.

Understanding the lines of authority is essential in combat because a military unit needs to fight as a team against the enemy, and a team must have a leader. The centurion, who commanded one hundred Roman soldiers, understood lines of authority. He approached Jesus and asked Him to heal a paralyzed servant who was miles away. The centurion asked Jesus to just say the word, knowing that his servant would be healed. He said to Jesus, "For I am a man under authority, with soldiers under me; and I say to one, 'Go,' and he goes, and to another, 'Come,' and he comes . . ." (Matthew 8:9). The centurion recognized that Jesus was under authority to His Father and so felt safe in making his request.

My attitude toward authority made it easy for me to recognize and salute an officer and carry out different commands, because this had been my way in civilian life. This commitment of submission to authority and team-work made it easy for the Air Force to promote me. As I learned my job in the Air Force, I was promoted several times to a higher rank. The promotions indicated that I was doing my job to the satisfaction of my commander. Promotions are a sign of respect and authority because they call for more responsibility.

As my military training drew to a close in November 1943, I knew we were prepared to go into battle overseas. Our crew had been assigned to the Eighth Air Force in England. After finishing our assignment at Rapid City, South Dakota, we went to Kearney, Nebraska, to fly a B-17 bomber overseas to England. On the way, we flew to an air base near Miami, Florida.

As we left Miami, soon after being airborne, we nearly suffered a midair collision. Another airplane entered our assigned airspace and we almost collided. We were so close that we could see a couple of faces in the windows of their airplane. They had entered our airspace with no authority to be where they were, and the result was almost disastrous.

Spiritual Authority

The Air Force promoted me as I learned to use responsibly the authority they gave me. Later in life I discovered that God, in a sense, promotes His people as they learn how to walk in spiritual authority (see Luke 19:17). If we learn to be faithful in a little, He will give us more, as one pastor learned.

I was with a group of spiritual leaders going to a worldwide charismatic meeting in Helsinki, Finland. While waiting in a New York airport, one of the pastors told me that his congregation had trouble accepting him as a prophet.

I asked him, "Do you tell them you are a prophet?"

"Yes," he said.

I said, "Don't tell them you are a prophet. Let them tell you! Others who are knowledgeable in the gifts of the Holy Spirit will confirm your spiritual gifts."

The pastor was learning that spiritual authority is given and acknowledged; it cannot be taken and imposed.

Shortly after I returned from Finland, a pastor from Texas asked me for guidelines on how to conduct a Spirit-led council meeting. I suggested using the three ingredients of prophecy: encouragement, upbuilding and consolation (see 1 Corinthians 14:3).

I challenge all Christians to include these three ingredients in their relationships. Would not the Gospel truly be honored if we looked at others the way God does? Meetings at church would be fun and exciting as we encouraged one another!

My Texan friend called me immediately after the council meeting, excited that they had a breakthrough! He said, "The meeting was so different. Our council meetings generally end late at night with our usual disagreements. Tonight, as we encouraged one another, the meeting became more personal. The church business was the smallest part of the meeting—we just united in the Holy Spirit by sharing and approving one another! It was a great council meeting."

My friend was learning the nature of spiritual authority. The apostle Paul writes about "our authority, which the Lord gave for building you up and not for destroying you . . ." (2 Corinthians 10:8). Spiritual authority has a protective, building value and makes true freedom possible.

The Bible describes two positions of authority: worldly and spiritual. Jesus describes how they are exercised:

> "You know that the rulers of the Gentiles lord it over them, and their great men exercise authority over them. It shall not be so among you; but whoever would be great among you must be your servant, and whoever would be first among you must be your slave."

> Matthew 20:25–27

Worldly authority reveals itself through wars, terrorism and many other acts of power that bring tension, stress and anxiety. It is born out of a self-serving spirit that cannot comprehend anything but personal satisfaction. Worldly authority is not willing to learn, because it believes it has already arrived at its fullness.

God calls us to recognize that submitting to spiritual authority involves responsibility and consequences. Paul writes to the saints at Rome, "For there is no authority except from God, and those that exist have been instituted by God" (Romans 13:1).

Jesus said, "All authority in heaven and on earth has been given to me" (Matthew 28:18). The same spiritual authority that was given to Jesus is the authority we receive when we are born into the spiritual realm. There is only One who has the final authority in all spiritual warfare—God!

Not understanding spiritual authority has put Christians at a disadvantage in spiritual warfare. Because of our lack of knowledge about spiritual authority, Satan has wreaked havoc upon countless churches, homes and societies. If we stand up and challenge Satan in the name of Jesus, he dare not usurp what rightfully belongs to us. This is why a growing Christian needs to learn the difference between good and bad authority.

Good and Bad Authority

Good spiritual authority knows how to fight spiritual warfare. It arises out of humility, submission and obedience to God. Spiritual authority is normally not imposed but responded to.

Jesus taught and walked in authority because He was focused and obedient to do His Father's will. The common people recognized that Jesus' spiritual authority was always for their well-being. But many Israelites at that time expected a leader who would wage a physical war to overcome Rome. Many Jews wanted a war that included blood and death for the Romans. They thought that a physical war would solve their problems.

Jesus knew that physical war was not the answer. His weapons were spiritual truths that would replace worldly mindsets. He came to lead spiritual warfare against the powers of darkness that produced legalistic thinking and held people in bondage. His authority for this warfare came from His Father.

God gives people a will so that they can choose either to follow or to reject His leadership. Good authority gives others the same freedom, providing clear choices, consistent leadership and sensitivity for others. Good spiritual authority produces warriors who are confident, free, responsive, loving and open to walking in faith. Good spiritual authority always draws out the potential in others, helping them to receive what God has provided for them.

Sometimes spiritual authority must be exercised to provide discipline and correction, and to maintain law and order. Jesus challenged the money-changers, the Pharisees and the scribes who were leading people astray. He saw that the Pharisees and scribes were hypocrites, laying heavy burdens on people. They did not practice what they were preaching. In other words, they were not walking it the way they were talking it. They were abusive in their authority.

I grew up thinking that correction was rejection. My father, after disciplining me, would reject me by ignoring me, giving me the silent treatment for several days. Because of my father's flawed discipline, I became defensive. It took the power of the Holy Spirit's renewal to teach me that correction is not rejection but is simply suggesting a better way of doing things. Now I appreciate it when someone critiques me. The writer of Proverbs says, "Whoever loves discipline loves knowledge, but he who hates reproof is stupid" (Proverbs 12:1).

Abusive authority reveals itself in dictatorship or a controlling spirit. This type of leadership, whether in a country, church or home, breeds rebellion. It creates suspicion and distrust, robbing the followers of dignity, self-worth, joy and productivity. In Germany and Italy we have seen dictators who are prime examples of abusive authority. The people suffer while the authorities prosper!

When a family is run dictator-style, there is always abuse—emotional, verbal or physical. The family either becomes totally dependent on the person in authority and loses self-worth or, as soon as possible, flees to some other place for refuge.

Abusive authority will use any method to crush opposition because it does not value the opinions or needs of others. It is a bully authority. The attitude of the dictator or control spirit is "My way or the highway!"

This type of authority is often exercised by church councils and congregations, forcing good pastors to leave after a short time in the parish. It is a subtle expression of spiritual warfare, led by control spirits. If a parish, in malice, changes pastors every two or three years, I would suspect that a deceitful control spirit powered by Satan lurks behind the scene. It is a comingled spirit of pride and rebellion.

Mediocre authority, on the other hand, often produces followers who are laid-back, double-minded, confused procrastinators with no direction in life. Instead of being actors in God's plan, they end up reacting to unexpected situations. They lack vision or a willingness to seize the opportunities God provides. Many churches are guilty in this area of leadership, as evidenced by their lack of vision, growth and spiritual authority.

In churches like these, council meetings are more concerned about the status quo than about asking God for direction. Their agenda is focused on meeting the budget. Their evangelism thrust is nil, and they are satisfied with their traditionalism. This type of authority lacks an understanding of spiritual warfare.

John tells us, "The reason the Son of God appeared was to destroy the works of the devil" (1 John 3:8). To *destroy* means "to end something by breaking up, tearing down, ruining and spoiling what was before." God sent Jesus to defeat the works of the devil through the Word, good spiritual authority and leadership.

God wants to free His people to build His kingdom. Our part is to hear Him and do what He says. The psalmist writes, "Unless the LORD builds the house, those who build it labor in vain . . ." (Psalm 127:1). God provides the spiritual authority and tools to accomplish His work.

I have discovered that churches that are growing spiritually and numerically are focused on God and allowing His spiritual authority to flow. Their meetings, Bible studies and all activities are centered around the Holy Spirit building the Church. This requires learning spiritual authority! If we are active frontline soldiers under spiritual authority, we become dangerous to evil.

The Authority of God's Word

I have learned that if I am going to walk in spiritual authority and become dangerous to evil, I need to know God's Word. God spoke and the world was created. The Word is creative and powerful!

Surveys show that the average Christian spends very little time reading the Bible. A Scripture-emaciated army will not come to maturity nor win spiritual battles for lost souls! A Holy Spirit-led army that knows the Word will overwhelm the enemy in spiritual warfare.

I know God is faithful to His Word. There have been times in my life when His Word was the rock I stood upon while everything else was crumbling. I have discovered the authority of God's Word in spiritual warfare. The Word is given by God that His people might prove to be an unstoppable force. It has been battlefield-tested down through the centuries with great results!

The writer to the Hebrews writes, "For the word of God is living and active, sharper than any two-edged sword, piercing to the division of soul and spirit, of joints and marrow, and discerning the thoughts and intentions of the heart" (Hebrews 4:12).

Knowing the Word helps us to become God's warriors! If we are eager to know God through His Word, we need to study and fellowship with those who are of the same desire and spirit. I learn God's Word not by memorization but by reading a specific section each day for thirty days. As I read the Word, I observe two emphases.

One emphasis is for my head. I need to absorb knowledge of what God has done throughout history. For example: "In those days the Philistines gathered their forces for war, to fight against Israel . . ." (1 Samuel 28:1).

The other emphasis is for my heart, where the Word applies to my life. For example: "And I am sure that he who began a good work in you will bring it to completion at the day of Jesus Christ" (Philippians 1:6). This Scripture is a heart-principle and promise that God's people can claim personally. I have prayed this promise for many people, in spite of their negative circumstances. God is bigger than any of our circumstances, and He is always ready to fulfill His promises!

When I started studying the Bible for the first time, I began by reading Paul's letter to the Philippians for thirty days in a row. As I read the letter over and over, it became imprinted on my mind. When I think of Philippians today, I see in my mind the whole letter printed out. It is a good way and place to start. Now it is the responsibility of the Holy Spirit to bring verses to light so that they become heart-truth to me.

When I pray, claiming a Scripture verse for a situation that is confronting me, God honors His Word and the verse becomes heart-truth to me! The Word in my heart confirms that I have applied God's truth and been obedient to Him.

The psalmist says, "I have laid up thy word in my heart, that I might not sin against thee" (Psalm 119:11). Jesus, after His forty-day fast, answered Satan's three temptations with, "It is written" (see Matthew 4). If we know the Word, we can stand in the face of any temptation, trial or enemy and our answer will be the same: "It is written" (Luke 4:1–14).

The Word of God needs to be the foundation for our thought patterns or else we will build on airy presuppositions. God gave us His Word to teach and guide us, confirming our faith and obedience as we follow the Holy Spirit. As we study the Scripture, it challenges us to faith, love and the fulfilling of His vision, for it is God revealing Himself to us.

The Authority of Christ's Name

In reading the Scriptures, I have discovered that Christ has given us the power of attorney to use His name. He proclaims:

"And these signs will accompany those who believe: in my name they will cast out demons; they will speak in new tongues; they will pick up serpents, and if they drink any deadly thing, it will not hurt them; they will lay their hands on the sick, and they will recover."

Mark 16:17–18

With the name of Jesus comes all the divine power that was present at creation. He has not changed, and neither has His power. It is extremely important that we learn when, where and how to use His name in spiritual warfare.

The first time that God led me to use the authority of Jesus' name, it was to rebuke a demon that had been subtly destroying a home and marriage. A couple with three children came to me for help because they were on the verge of getting a divorce. Their three teenage children were giving them trouble, and the couple had no idea what to do.

After counseling together, we prayed for God's insight as to what was causing their problems. The names of two demons came to my mind as we prayed. I shared with the couple what God seemed to be saying, and they agreed that the demons mentioned could be the cause of their problems.

I took authority over the demons in the name of Jesus and forbade them to harass this family. I also asked God to mute the swearing of their children.

When I saw them again two weeks later, they both said that their relationship was changing. She said, "Our relationship is as if we have gone back to our courting days. Our children have quit swearing. Our home has changed because of prayer!"

I now understand that the power of Jesus' name is the power of attorney. When we speak in submission to Jesus, who submits to the Father, all the power of the Godhead is backing up our prayer.

The Authority of Jesus' Blood

We said earlier that good authority is protective. The blood of Christ Jesus is a wonderful picture of this principle. Christians do not like to talk about His blood, either because they lack understanding or because they have been deceived by the enemy. But as soldiers involved in spiritual warfare we need to know the meaning, power and purpose of the blood of Jesus.

This truth is revealed in Exodus when God cautions His people to put the blood of the lamb on the doorpost and the lintel of the house in which they eat the lamb. It was the Lord's Passover, and the plague was to fall upon all Egyptians to destroy them. Those who put up the blood of the lamb were passed over by the destroyer because the blood was their protection (see Exodus 12:1–32). Just as the blood protected the Israelites dwelling in Egypt, so will the blood that Jesus shed at the cross protect us today, because it is the seal of our adoption under the New Covenant.

Jesus' blood is the first thing I bring into a confrontation with demons. By it I cleanse my heart and put the whole situation under the protection and authority of God. The blood of Jesus is a reminder to the powers of darkness that they were defeated at the cross. I would not consider doing the ministry I do in my Christian walk if I was not confident in Jesus and the protection of His blood.

The apostle John writes, "And they have conquered him [Satan] by the blood of the Lamb and by the word of their testimony, for they loved not their lives even unto death" (Revelation 12:11).

Every day as I pray for the members of our family, I bind the powers of darkness in Jesus' name. I release the blood of Jesus for our protection. I ask God to prosper my little tribe with His presence, and that His perfect plan and purpose for the day be worked out in our lives.

The Authority of the Keys

I was filled with joy when I read Jesus' words: "I will give you the keys of the kingdom of heaven, and whatever you bind on earth shall be bound in heaven, and whatever you loose on earth shall be loosed in heaven" (Matthew 16:19). I became aware that Jesus gives us two keys to go with His authority for fighting in spiritual warfare. One key is to bind the enemy; the other key is to loose the Holy Spirit into any situation.

Just as a key locks the door to a home, trapping an intruder outside, God gives us spiritual authority against the enemy who wants to destroy our lives. That is the key to bind the intruder in Jesus' name.

When the intruder is bound, we take the second key and loose the Holy Spirit upon him. That is like calling 911; the police respond and take the intruder away. Be assured that the moment we bind the powers of darkness on earth, they are bound in heaven. The moment we take authority in Jesus' name and loose the Holy Spirit, truth and understanding are released to our part of the battlefield.

63

When Satan was cast out of heaven, he encouraged many angels to go with him. These fallen angels are called demons. They are spiritual beings with a job description—to destroy everything that God made good. Jesus recognized Satan, the head demon, and others that we are called to overcome.

The apostle Paul writes, "For we are not contending against flesh and blood, but against the principalities, against the powers, against the world rulers of this present darkness, against the spiritual hosts of wickedness in the heavenly places" (Ephesians 6:12).

One January night I received a call from a family that was experiencing demonic problems. They asked if Betty and I would come over. It was a bitterly cold night with nearly two feet of snow on the ground, but we responded yes.

The Holy Spirit began to stir my mind how to meet their needs. They needed someone with spiritual authority to walk around their land and claim it for the Lord. God told Joshua, "Every place that the sole of your foot will tread upon I have given to you, as I promised to Moses" (Joshua 1:3). Now He was telling me the same thing.

The husband and I walked around the outside of their land, praising and singing as we waded through the deep snow. We claimed the land based on God's promise to Joshua. We asked God to raise a spiritual barrier of protection around the family and land.

Two days later the lady was washing dishes when she looked out the kitchen window and God showed her His protection. In the Spirit, she saw demonic forces restrained from crossing the line that had been made by the Holy Spirit. She saw a large black figure sitting on a black horse.

The rider was looking at the house but was restrained by an invisible line.

When we claim in the name of Jesus the ground that we have been given, the powers of darkness are forbidden to intrude. I have walked around my home and claimed it for the Lord. I was pleasantly surprised the first time I claimed the promise—not only that the spiritual promise works, but that spiritual blessings always come with the promise of more freedom.

To attain this freedom we must engage in spiritual warfare. A free Christian can draw closer to God than one in bondage to worldly habits. Satan, knowing that, will use every ruse and deception to keep God's people ignorant and in bondage.

Some itinerant exorcists once tried to cast out a demon in the name of Jesus. But they did not know Christ, only about Him. As they tried to cast out the evil spirit, it answered them, "'Jesus I know, and Paul I know; but who are you?'" (Acts 19:15). The man who had the evil spirit leaped on the seven exorcists and beat them up (see Acts 19:13–16). Battling demons calls for knowing and walking in the spiritual authority we have in Christ!

The Power to Battle Demons

In spiritual warfare we need to remember that not everything negative is the work of Satan. A lot of what gets blamed on demons is really the principle of sowing and reaping in action. If we sow wickedness or negativity, that is what we will reap (see Galatians 6:7–8). There is, however, no avoiding the truth that Satan is as real as the world and our flesh.

When I was new to spiritual warfare and had not yet learned about the Christian's authority, my wife and I encountered a demon.

Betty had started speaking at various women's groups concerning the death of our son in Vietnam. She shared how God's presence and grace were seeing us through this tragic ordeal. After she had spoken in a small town, a woman handed her a crumpled piece of paper. She would not look Betty in the eye but immediately slinked away.

After Betty came home, she pulled the small scrap of paper out of her pocket. In a tiny scribble, difficult to read, was this woman's phone number and the word "help." Being new in the walk of faith but eager to please God, we talked about seeing her.

The next day Betty called her and set up a meeting. The woman sounded fearful and confused, but eager to come to our home if it meant she could be helped.

The following day this well-dressed woman rang our doorbell. My wife greeted her and immediately brought her to our family room. After a short conversation Betty asked what was troubling her.

Slouching in a chair, not looking at us, she responded, "Set me free." She would not divulge what she wanted to be set free from, but we laid our hands on her and prayed. After praying and talking for some time with no obvious relief for her, I left and went into the bedroom to pray.

Kneeling by the bed I prayed, *O Lord, we are new in faith and do not know how to help this woman.*

Just then Betty came into the room and said, "Isn't there some place in the Bible where it tells us to lay on hands and cast out demons?"

I replied, "I don't know, but we can give it a try."

We went to the woman and again laid our hands on her. Betty said, "If there is a demon, you come out of her right now." The woman heaved a big sigh of relief and immediately seemed totally different. Her attitude changed. She was able to make eye contact with us. We finished our coffee, and this woman left our home free! God had met her need.

Little did we know what was in store for us. My wife is normally cheerful in the morning, but the next day she appeared morose and fearful. She would not open the blinds and kept the drapes drawn. Her attitude seemed to be as dark and dreary as our closed, dark home.

When it came time for me to go to work, she begged me not to go. She did not want to be left alone. Fear showed in her face. I told her that I had to go to work but that I would keep her in prayer during the day.

The next two weeks seemed like hell on earth as we unknowingly lived with a demon of fear. Finally we met with someone who was knowledgeable about demons, and Betty dealt with the demon of fear. She immediately changed back into her usual self, set free from the demon's influence.

We were getting a "hands-on" lesson in spiritual authority and warfare. Soon after this I read the Scripture, "Do not be hasty in the laying on of hands . . ." (1 Timothy 5:22). The above verse normally applies to ordaining a pastor, but the principle of being hasty in laying on of hands applies to many spiritual situations. In this case a demon had left the woman and chosen my wife to harass.

Although God allowed this to happen, He protected us. He displayed His sovereignty and used that struggle to show us how badly we needed to learn more about spiritual authority.

Spirits Are Subject to Us

God has universal and unlimited power over His creation. He who created the universe is capable of keeping it on course. Many times I have been involved in spiritual warfare and had to depend on God's authority over demons. Not once has He failed.

In the early 1970s, a couple who had been married for about three years came to the church seeking help. They had heard that North Heights Lutheran Church was a charismatic church that ministered to all areas of spiritual need. The wife came from several generations of spiritual mystics involved in things like fortune-telling, telefax reading and palm reading. This couple was in the pastor's office, and the demons from her background were acting up, so Pastor Morris Vaagenes called and asked if I could come over.

The wife was normally a quiet woman but now was angry and belligerent. She had already taken a letter opener from the pastor's desk and tried to stab him. Once her husband and the pastor were finally able to calm her down, Pastor Vaagenes called me because he and I had together dealt with demons several times previously.

Entering the office, I saw a rather large woman—both tall and stocky— who had her back toward me. The pastor was behind his desk, and the woman was talking to her husband in a normal tone of voice.

Pastor Vaagenes described what had transpired and we immediately began to pray, preparing the way for the woman's deliverance. After prayer, Pastor Vaagenes walked around the desk to confront the demons.

As he spoke the demons began to bristle, as if they did not like the confrontation. The woman began to talk in a loud voice, denying that the pastor had any authority over her. He began to talk about the demons' defeat at the cross through the blood of Jesus and reminded them that, by the authority given through Jesus Christ, they had to obey and leave her.

The demons stiffened her body and she wiggled fiercely, showing that they were not going to come out without a fight. As she grew more violent I gently but firmly pinned her arms from behind to prevent her from hurting herself or us. Pastor Vaagenes continued to speak with authority, and she began coughing and gagging as if she were going to vomit. He spoke of the shed blood of Jesus and told the demons that, in Jesus' name, they had to come out now!

Suddenly her struggling stopped. Her body lost its tenseness, went limp, and I gently released my hold. The demons had left her! This battle between the powers of darkness and the Holy Spirit was over, as evidenced by her peace. We rejoiced with praise songs for we saw the power of Jesus' name and His blood. The demons had no choice but to surrender!

Rejoice That Your Names Are Written in Heaven

As I grew in confidence, God had me take another step of faith. I was called to a Sunday-through-Tuesday evangelistic crusade in North Dakota. When I arrived, the pastor greeted me with, "I did not want you here, but the committee on evangelism did."

I soon found out that he did not want any part of charismatic renewal because it was foreign to his seminary training. I moaned inside, *O Lord, what do You have in mind? The pastor does not want me here, but I know that You gave me a clear signal to come.*

The Holy Spirit spoke to my mind, *You do your part, and I will do Mine.* I knew that my part was to deliver what the Holy Spirit would reveal to me. I made up my mind to do that regardless of the circumstances and leave the rest up to Him.

The Sunday morning services flowed smoothly. There were several worship leaders who were free in the leading of the service, singing renewal songs. The evening service was even more liberated, with a number of people giving personal testimony about their relationship with God. (Personal testimony is not normally given in a Lutheran church.)

I talked about God's desire to fill His people with Holy Spirit power and how the Holy Spirit had changed my life when I discovered that He is for real. After my message I gave an invitation to come to the altar and be baptized with the Holy Spirit. About forty people responded to the call and came forward to kneel at the altar. I prayed for the pastor, then asked him to join me in laying hands on the first two people at the altar rail.

We prayed together so that he could get an idea of how to minister the baptism with the Holy Spirit. I then went to the other end of the altar and started praying for people while he continued from his end.

God did not disappoint us! The people were not inhibited by their friends. They were being touched by the Holy Spirit, as was evidenced by strange tongues and tears of joy as the people experienced a new freedom.

I asked a young woman about twenty years old if she wanted to be filled with Holy Spirit power. She responded in a low, condescending voice, "Who do you think you are?"

Discerning a demon, I put my mouth near her ear and began to speak softly so as not to disturb other people. I said, "I have been sent by Jesus to set this girl free from you." I bound the demon in Jesus' name. I then asked God to cover the situation with the protective blood of Jesus, loosed the Holy Spirit and prayed that the demon would come out quietly. But no, it had to let out a shriek before coming out (as they often did for Jesus Himself).

As the demon left her, the young woman slumped against the altar rail, exhausted but free! As soon as she gained some composure, I prayed for the baptism in the Holy Spirit. It was obvious that she received Him, as she broke forth in a new language and tears of joy. She was free!

After closing the service, the pastor came over to me with tears flowing down his cheeks. He said, "I have never prayed for my people like this before. My ministry was new tonight. I felt so close to God. I am so thankful you came!"

I was reminded of Jesus' words in Luke 10:20: "Do not rejoice that the spirits submit to you, but rejoice that your names are written in heaven" (NIV). Now *that* is victory in spiritual warfare!

Holy Spirit training means that we never stop learning. I was teachable and eager to learn. The Holy Spirit was ready to take me to my next lesson where I would learn about Satan's propaganda warfare.

4

SATAN'S PROPAGANDA WAR

The Battle for the Mind

In any war, the fight begins with a battle for the minds of the soldiers and civilians involved. During World War II, the Japanese used radio broadcasts by a woman called Tokyo Rose to discourage American soldiers, sailors and airmen. Her shows were carefully designed to ruin their morale.

I listened to Tokyo Rose's European counterpart several times. She was called Axis Sally and was sponsored by the Germans. Her job was to make us homesick and tired of war. She played many sentimental songs that focused on our loved ones back home. I enjoyed the songs but was not diverted from the job I was called to do: to help defeat Germany and Italy.

A soldier needs to have a disciplined mind that is focused on the strategy to obtain victory. That is why I usually listened to the BBC (British Broadcasting Company), which gave our Armed Forces a positive approach to the war. Though Axis Sally tried playing with my mind, I refused to give in to her "stinking thinking," which could have made me weak and vulnerable.

The first time we were attacked by German fighter planes, they came from the direction of the sun, so I had difficulty seeing them. One fighter plane came at our bomber with two lights flashing on its wings. The lights were muzzle-flash. He was shooting right at me! I returned fire with my two 50-caliber machine guns. Every fifth shell I fired was a tracer that revealed the paths of my bullets. I could see at an instant the direction I was aiming, which was vital. In combat with German fighters, time was of the essence; everything happened so fast! As the firefight between us unfolded, I understood the reason for all my training. I had been through many mock battles; this was the real thing. Now my head was clear and my hands moved almost automatically. I could never have done my job if my head was full of Axis Sally's chatter.

In spiritual warfare we encounter our true enemy. This battle leaves no room in our minds for stinking thinking.

Stinking Thinking

Stinking thinking comes out of a mind that is not submitted to God. Its thought patterns are based in pride. A proud mind is not concerned about the spiritual propaganda war, because a prideful person has already been invaded and conquered. As we watch TV and read various kinds of worldly literature, we are under attack by half-truths. Once we accept these half-truths, they become part of the foundation for our thought patterns.

Satan's strategy is to infiltrate our minds with the disease of stinking thinking. Through stinking thinking, Satan assaults my mind in various ways; perhaps with the thought that I am too busy to read the Bible, or by words that I will later wish I had not spoken. Sometimes he tempts me to take actions that come out of emotions, without thinking of the consequences. People seem to become more irritating. Drivers cut me off in traffic. It becomes more difficult to get along with my wife. These hassles are often the subtle, deceitful work of Satan's propaganda war.

Victory in spiritual warfare requires a departure from stinking thinking. We need a whole new mindset—one of discerning God's will. This makes it imperative that we understand how our minds function. The apostle Paul tells us:

> For though we live in the world we are not carrying on a worldly war, for the weapons of our warfare are not worldly but have divine power to destroy strongholds. We destroy arguments and every proud obstacle to the knowledge of God, and take every thought captive to obey Christ.
>
> 2 Corinthians 10:3–5

It is urgent that we learn how to "take every thought captive to obey Christ." God challenges us to become accountable and responsible for making the right choices. The choices we make determine the outcome of our spiritual battles. Not understanding how our minds work can

75

open the door to sinful thought patterns. This results in making our minds vulnerable to a full-scale attack.

If our minds are the battlefield, how does the battle start? Spiritual warfare starts when conflicting thoughts enter our minds—God's pure thoughts and Satan's propaganda. Who will rule: God or Satan?

When a thought comes from the Holy Spirit, it will be confirmed by a healthy Christian conscience. From there the thought goes to the conscious mind, where it comes into conflict with an opposing thought from our self-centered old nature. Here is where the spiritual warfare becomes intense. The self-centered old nature, encouraged by Satan, fights against relinquishing its control to the Holy Spirit.

Space for Rent

"Candid Camera" is a TV show in which people are filmed by a hidden camera but are unaware that they are being taped. Once Allen Funk, producer of the show, posed as an owner of a candy store in New York. He posted a sign that read, "No small change given." As customers purchased candy, Mr. Funk refused to give any small change. The hidden camera recorded their reactions.

Several customers who bought candy and received no small change were upset and indignant. They could not believe Mr. Funk had the audacity to withhold their change, in spite of a sign indicating that no small change would be given. A man about 35 years old spent $6.20 for candy and gave Mr. Funk a ten dollar bill. Mr. Funk politely gave him three dollars in change. The man looked at the three dollars and then at Mr. Funk, shrugged his shoulders, turned and started walking out with his purchase, less his eighty cents change.

Mr. Funk called him back and asked him, "Why weren't you upset when I didn't give you the small change?" The man made a comment I will never forget: "I refuse to rent out space in my head for eighty cents!"

The mind is the battlefield! The enemy comes disguised as an angel of light and challenges us to rent space in our head. This may be through pride, lust, greed, unforgiveness, gossip or any variety of thoughts that assault our minds.

If we struggle with overeating, the battle over our "space for rent" might go something like this: We have eaten until we are satisfied, but Satan keeps tempting us through our thoughts: "Have another helping. You deserve seconds on dessert. It won't hurt to have a little more. That's the best cake you've had in a long time!"

The Holy Spirit counters with the thought: *You do not need more food. You are the temple of God. Please ask Me for help and I will give you power and strength to counter temptation.*

Both of these thoughts come from outside our conscious mind—one by Satan's temptation, the other by inspiration of the Holy Spirit. Then, by an act of our will, we choose the thought pattern we wish to follow. Will it be the Holy Spirit, who leads us to self-acceptance and joyful lives, or Satan, who leads to death of our spirits and souls? The struggle between listening to a godly conscience or Satan *is* spiritual warfare!

To keep the enemy from renting space in our heads, we need an ongoing awareness of the Lord. God will give us His thoughts and show us His way of dealing with any situation that confronts us.

How Thoughts Lead to Sin

Our enemy, knowing that he can subtly influence our choices, tries to lead us into sin. The writer of Genesis tells it like it is: "And if you do not do well, sin is couching at the door; its desire is for you, but you must master it" (Genesis 4:7).

Sin is always ready to be our next thought. Its desire to rule us makes a sinful thought clamor aggressively to rent space in our minds. But God challenges us to discern sinful thoughts and master them by rejecting them.

For years I was under the impression that every wicked thought I would have was sin. That understanding made being a Christian extremely difficult and filled with failure. When my thoughts, encouraged by Satan and assisted by my imagination, develop into a consistent negative pattern, then I am in sin. But if I take them captive immediately, crushing them before they become a pattern, they are not sin—simply attacks by my enemy. Because of my ignorance, I felt helpless to control my thought life. I tried to ignore sins that today I deal with immediately. I was involved in spiritual warfare and did not know it!

Sin is anything that stands in opposition to God's character, plan and purpose for His creation. Sin, by its nature, causes separation from God. When we are tempted by self-centered thoughts and we act on those thoughts, we fall into sin. The apostle James puts it very succinctly: "But each person is tempted when he is lured and enticed by his own desire. Then desire when it has conceived gives birth to sin; and sin when it is full-grown brings forth death" (James 1:14–15).

To *conceive* means "to form or develop lustful thoughts and images in our minds and imaginations." The imagination can be used in powerful ways, to accomplish either God's work or Satan's. When we begin to dwell on unhealthy thoughts, we are committing sin.

Three Kinds of Lust

Satan's strategy is to challenge us deceitfully with lust, materialism, pride and power. The apostle John put it this way:

> For all that is in the world, the lust of the flesh and the lust of the eyes and the pride of life, is not of the Father but is of the world. And the world passes away, and the lust of it; but he who does the will of God abides for ever.
>
> 1 John 2:16–17

The lust of the flesh, lust of the eyes (materialism) and pride are Satan's primary means of preventing us from doing God's will. These unholy things always battle with our consciences. They are like spies; their purpose is to infiltrate our thought patterns and slyly establish themselves.

When we rent space to Satan, our minds wander to thought patterns of lusting for the flesh. It leads down a road of guilt and despair, producing consequences that are beyond our imaginations. Lustful thought patterns have destroyed several television evangelists, ruined many ministries and torn apart countless marriages and homes. Multitudes of illegitimate children are born out of wedlock due to lusting for the flesh.

The way I contend with the lust of the flesh is to immediately start thanking God for creating whatever I have started lusting for. If the object is female, I thank

God for her beauty and think of her in terms of being a friend's sister or someone's mother. It is hard to lust after a woman while talking to God about her. He never approves. When my mind is focused on God, there is no room for sinful thoughts.

I would not want to jeopardize my relationship with God by a foolish act, so I also try to avoid situations where there would be a possibility of being subjected to Satan's propaganda.

Skiing Downhill

A friend told me how he started an affair by flirting with his secretary. He described his lusting as skiing downhill after an ice storm. He said, "Once I started lusting it seemed that I could not stop."

At first, he reasoned that no one would find out about what he was thinking. He did not take every thought captive for Christ. But after he flirted a couple of times, she began to respond to him with suggestive humor. My friend had already rented space in his head to lustful thoughts, so he urged his secretary to make a deeper commitment to him.

When he called her into his office to dictate letters, he often leaned over to smell her perfume. Once while in a close proximity to her, after checking the letter he dictated, he kissed her on the neck. The next time she was in his office he kissed her again. She reciprocated; both had responded to lust.

As they struggled with renting space in their heads to the enemy, their consciences told them that what was happening would have bad consequences. But by an act of their wills, they gave in to lust and overrode their consciences. Their work began to show signs that their minds were not focused on their jobs. Mistakes began showing in her computer work. He made a wrong decision that cost the company several million dollars. His and her minds were both focused on the excitement of this developing affair; they were compromising their consciences.

The result of such compromise is that both sides lose. After several weeks, the relationship became more torrid. He suggested going to a nearby motel for lunch. The power of lust had become too great for them to overcome without God's help. The inevitable happened.

Their spouses eventually found out about the adultery. Both the man and woman lost their jobs with the company. Both ended up divorced. He remarried, and she became a single mom—all because of lust propaganda. Neither of them knew how to take their thoughts captive to the will of Christ Jesus!

Lusting of the Eyes

Just lusting for the flesh brings myriads of problems; so does the materialistic lusting of the eyes. This unholy lusting for *things* leads to credit-card abuse, bankruptcy, guilt, hopelessness, despondency and envy, along with a plethora of other related emotions and problems. A greedy thought-pattern of lust will destroy us, because we are never satisfied with what we have.

Pride of Life

Pride brings a struggle between people: Who is right and who is wrong? Many divorces come about because of pride. What else can happen when neither spouse is willing to yield? Pride, whether it be in the private, social or political scene, destroys relationships, which are the very fabric of society. Anger gets us into trouble; pride *keeps* us in trouble!

Sometimes pride appears as a struggle for power over others. At home or at the office, it often takes the form of manipulation. Other times the struggle is more blatant. Why do people spend millions of dollars to get elected to a political office when the salary is far below what they spent to get elected? It is worth thinking about.

I have discovered that if Satan's propaganda cannot get into my mind, he will try to hit me in my emotions. His goal is to lead me into acts of sin, resulting in disunity and separation from God.

Victory over Satan's Propaganda

The following five spiritual principles have helped me discern where conflicting thoughts are coming from. Knowing the quality of the thoughts and where they originated helps me take my thoughts captive to obey Christ.

1. *Would I be willing to stand up and loudly shout this thought to my spouse, family or a passerby?* Or would I be ashamed of the thought?

2. *Is there a Bible verse related to this thought?* It is imperative to know spiritual truth as a foundation for all of life. Paul tells us, "Guard the truth that has been entrusted to you by the Holy Spirit who dwells within us" (2 Timothy 1:14). One of the ways the Lord defeated Satan was by knowing Scripture. Jesus simply stated, "It is written" (see Matthew 4:4).

This calls for us to know the Word and to use it properly by asking the Holy Spirit to bring to our minds the fitting words for every situation. Jesus said, "It is the spirit that gives life, the flesh is of no avail; the words that I have spoken to you are spirit and life" (John 6:63). When I entered into Holy Spirit training for spiritual warfare I became aware of how the enemy attacks me through my mind. Satan will attempt to make God's truth the first casualty, by trying to keep me too busy to read the Bible. My foundation for life then comes from worldly sources, which keep me spiritually weak and open to all kinds of temptations. If Satan can keep me from reading the Bible, he subtly controls my life.

In the Depression days of the late 1920s and 1930s, many men were out of work with no jobs available. Eggs were ten cents a dozen, but no one had a dime. It was a tough time for the whole country, and many people lived on the bare necessities of life. One of the ways some people met a need was to take a bottle of ketchup and mix it with hot water to make a thin tomato soup. Ketchup soup was not very nourishing, but people thought, "This is better than nothing." The soup had form but lacked the essence and ingredients of the real thing.

Just as that thin soup could not really nourish, irregular Scripture reading produces spiritual anemia. Just as the body needs solid food on a consistent basis, our spirits need a steady diet of God's solid truth. If we do not feed our spirits with God's Word and prayer, they become malnourished.

God's Word is our guide in all spiritual warfare. The Word contains the how-to's of warfare: where the battles are fought, where the power comes from to defeat the enemy and the strategies for spiritual victories. The Word, quickened by the Holy Spirit, can perform great surgery—cutting away sin and whatever holds us in bondage.

You see, the Word of God is also an offensive weapon against Satan. According to Ephesians 6, it is our only offensive weapon. The author of Hebrews writes, "For the word of God is living and active, sharper than any two-edged sword, piercing to the division of soul and spirit, of joints and marrow, and discerning the thoughts and intentions of the heart" (Hebrews 4:12). God's Word is used to make our enemy retreat!

3. *Does the thought bring honor to God and also to me?* When I was a teenager, going out with my friends, my father said, "Remember that you are a Denny!" He was implying that the name commanded honor and respect in the area where we lived. He did not want me to dishonor his name. Nor should we dishonor the name of Christ.

The most visible dishonor to Christ is when a respected Christian is caught in a compromising situation; when a pastor takes advantage of a person in a counseling session or when a known Christian in government work fails to do what his conscience tells him is right. But the enemy works every day to trip me up so that I will sin, and every sin dishonors the name and mission of God!

4. *Is the thought negative or positive?* We live in a negative world, but the Holy Spirit gives us power to edify and encourage others.

Early one morning at a restaurant, a man saw a well-disciplined family of seven. They were obviously of a different race, and seemed to be of a different religion as well. The man had a positive thought: to buy their breakfasts unbeknownst to the family. He asked God for a sign; if they prayed over their meal when they were served, he would act on his inclination to bless them with a free breakfast. When they were served, they prayed. He paid for their meal on the way out, and left with the greater blessing that comes from giving.

5. *Is the thought convicting or condemning?* Conviction leads to repentance and forgiveness. Satan's ploy is to bring condemnation, which can steal away our security and peace in Christ. Condemnation is an invasion of self-centered thinking and low self-esteem. The result is a loss of hope, leading to despair.

A man once came to me weighed down with over a year's worth of condemnation. He thought that he had committed the unpardonable sin, the denial of the Holy Spirit. Needless to say, he had been renting space in his head to the enemy.

I shared with him that his concern about denying the Holy Spirit showed that he was not guilty of the crime. Satan had suggested the thought, he rented out space and bought the idea, and consequently he suffered condemnation. He went away from our conversation a free man in Christ, rather than a confused casualty of spiritual warfare.

The Need for Teamwork

World War II was a time God used to build a nation committed to teamwork. During the 1940s our nation came together in unity to win the war. There was one thought: "Work together—show the world that we are one in spirit." After completing my regular military training in September 1943, I was assigned to a bomber crew being formed at Rapid City, South Dakota. What a thrill to complete another step toward combat in Europe!

The ten men on my B-17 bomber crew had to learn teamwork, for in combat our lives depended on each other. Each of us had a position to fill on the big airplane. If one individual failed his part, the whole crew would be in jeopardy.

The training time at Rapid City was to teach us how to function as a team. Relationships were built among the ten men. We learned each other's strengths and weaknesses; physically, emotionally and spiritually. As a team, it was extremely important that we trust one another and be disciplined in following orders. The crew functioned as one being when we were in the air. It did not matter if you were a second lieutenant or a sergeant: We were more concerned about ability to perform than about rank.

Our days were also spent flying and learning the capabilities of the B-17. Often we flew low between the Black Hills. Flying at 300 to 400 feet above the ground, we saw farms and livestock flash by. Several times we flew low, then put the plane in a climb. When I looked back, I could see chickens being blown around from the propeller's blast.

Our three months flew by fast as we learned to support one another. Soon we had developed as a crew and were ready to take our places on the battle lines to bring home a victory!

Community

As in military teamwork, it is imperative that Christians learn to know and trust each other. My weekly schedule is built around three Bible studies: one on Tuesday, one on Thursday and one on Saturday morning. One study group has met for thirty years. We hold each other accountable to our responsibilities. If there is a need, several men are always available to help out. Many of the men are involved in different ministries, and they are capable of dealing with the enemy in any spiritual area.

God's strategy is to prepare His people against anything that might undermine them. By trust, faith, hope and obedience we can be rooted and grounded against any of the enemy's propaganda. But we cannot fight the battle for our minds by ourselves. We need Christian fellowship, the teamwork of other believers. With them we can focus on the good, godly thoughts that counteract Satan's propaganda. Together we can study the Bible, worship, engage in Christian conversation, share our lives and pray for one another.

A Cure for Unworthiness

My wife spent a season teaching a Bible study for high school and college students at our home on Monday nights. One night, a nineteen-year-old girl who had just moved from a neighboring state came for the first time.

Lisa (not her real name) had graduated from high school with average marks and had wanted to go to the local college. Her parents wanted her out of the house, so they agreed to pay her college tuition and expenses.

Lisa was average-looking but quite overweight. She said that, for most of her life, her parents had put her down as not capable of doing anything right. They, along with her siblings, were happy to have her gone from the home. Low self-esteem was stealing her life. Satan had convinced her that she would never amount to anything.

As she attended the Bible study, Lisa began to hear from her peer group that God loved her and that they

87

did, too. In spite of the affirmation, there was spiritual warfare going on in her mind—lies that told her she was not worthy.

A turning point in her life came on a holiday trip when the young people were water-skiing behind my boat. I tried 21 times to pull her up out of the water on the water skis, to no avail. The 22nd time she rose to her feet, and her life changed! The first thing out of her mouth when she came ashore was, "I am worthy—I can do something!"

Low self-esteem was defeated! Lisa had a new joy and confidence that she was capable of really living. Shortly after that she started to lose weight. After she graduated from college, she married and now has two grown boys. The enemy wanted to steal her quality of spiritual life through his propaganda—his stinking thinking. The battlefield was in her mind. But the Holy Spirit won the battle by surrounding her with a loving family of believers!

Disunity Is Death

Since World War II, I have discerned a satanic strategy: to make us a nation of individuals. As I reflect on the turmoil of the 1950s, 1960s and 1970s, I see how many people questioned their identities and roles in life. The Vietnam war, feminist rights and the Kent State University tragedy each spawned many mind-battles. The immigration of different ethnic groups and a variety of other social issues have been dividing the American culture. The issues of life now have a propensity to cause disunity and division. Disunity is at work!

Where there is disunity, there is a satanic power to destroy. The call of the enemy is to divide and conquer. Disharmony brings Satan a spiritual victory. He knows that disunity is freedom without responsibility—and without the protection of spiritual authority.

We as Christians need to realize that freedom is not a fleshly call to do what we want, but a call to be spiritually responsible. Jesus promises, "Again I say to you, if two of you agree on earth about anything they ask, it will be done for them by my Father in heaven" (Matthew 18:19).

Where two Christians agree, there is a spiritual power released to bring about what they agreed upon. That is why Satan hates unity. He wants a nation of individuals that are powerless; he seeks to destroy us through our disunity. God's power is to create and heal; it will always move us toward love and unity.

5

GUARDING OUR PERIMETERS

I stayed at several air force bases during the course of World War II. They all had one striking feature in common—a high barbed-wire fence, with guards posted to protect the boundary. The fence was an obstacle to anyone attempting to enter the air base. This is called a military perimeter and was especially important for American air bases overseas where there was greater risk of the enemy sneaking inside the perimeter.

In my travels since the war I have noticed large industrial complexes with high-wire fences. Electric power plants and city water plants have perimeters surrounding the buildings. Prisons also have large cement perimeters surrounding the compound. Many homeowners have fences encircling their lots. A fence is the owner declaring, "This is my property, and the only way in is through the gate."

Our souls and consciences are the gates to our lives. Satan keeps knocking at the gates of our thoughts, always trying to attack our minds with his evil propaganda. The need for perimeters around our minds becomes apparent when we engage in spiritual warfare. The apostle Paul warned us to take every thought captive to obey Christ (see 2 Corinthians 10:5).

I struggled with how to set up perimeters to protect my mind from Satan's evil propaganda. I knew that if I wanted to walk with God, my thoughts had to be protected from the enemy. Only with an ongoing awareness of God could I overcome Satan's wiles and defend against his attempts to infiltrate my thought life.

Satan's Strategy

I discovered that the strategy of the enemy is to ambush me. He lies in wait to attack me by surprise when I am not thinking about God. He tries to motivate me to say or do something against my soul and conscience. He will do whatever it takes to cause me to sin and bring disruption to God's plan for my life.

Satan comes at all of us through the simple things in life as he tries to divert us from doing what is right. Spiritual warfare is part of life so, naturally, the powers of darkness want to attack all relationships. This is why it is important to set perimeters around our relationships as we learn the fundamentals of spiritual warfare. The apostle John wrote, "We know that we are of God, and the whole world is in the power of the evil one" (1 John 5:19). *Evil* is anything that opposes God or His will. The following is a good example of Satan's sly methods.

A boy went to the local zoo, and on his way he picked up several rocks. Arriving at the polar bear compound, he waited until the bears were not watching. Then he threw a rock at a sleeping bear and hit it in the head. The bear did not know where the blow came from and assumed that a nearby bear had hit him. The injured bear then hit the next closest bear, and a fight was on! The heartless boy stood by and watched the bears fight.

In the same way, Satan attacks the perimeters of our minds with fiery darts and then steps back to watch the fallout.

The apostle Paul was watchful in protecting the perimeters of his mind. That is why he could write to the Ephesians about the armor of God, which is the spiritual battle-dress provided for God's soldiers. It is our attire for defense and offense. How can we protect our minds from Satan's evil propaganda? Paul gave the answer in his letter to the Ephesians. He wrote, "Besides all these, [take] the shield of faith, with which you can quench all the flaming darts of the evil one" (Ephesians 6:16).

The shield of faith is developed by our trust in God. This shield is forged as we experience God's faithfulness through the trials of life. Under heat and pressure, these times of victory are spiritually fused together to provide a shield of faith that stops the fiery darts of the enemy.

Fiery darts come in countless shapes and from innumerable ambushes: critical comments, humor at our expense, slander, sexual temptation, unholy anger and many more. Anything that is negative, puts us down or distracts us from our godly purpose is a fiery dart. If a dart invades our souls or consciences, we become spiritual casualties until we confront and deal with the wound.

If we are alert when the enemy shoots fiery darts toward us, the darts finds themselves embedded in our shields of faith. They are then quenched by the Holy Spirit and become harmless.

Galatians 5:22–23
The Fruit of the Spirit

John 10:10
1. Steal
2. Kill
3. Destroy

Romans 14:17
a. Joy   Nehemiah 8:10
b. Peace   Philippians 4:7
c. Righteousness   Romans 10:1–4

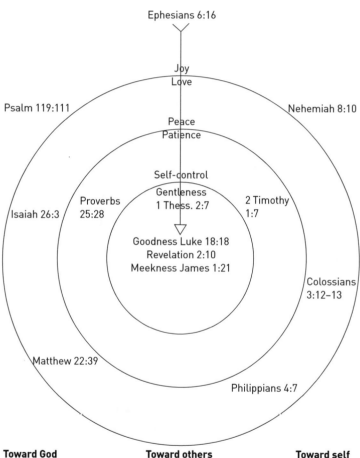

Ephesians 6:16

Joy
Love

Psalm 119:111

Peace
Patience

Nehemiah 8:10

Self-control
Gentleness
1 Thess. 2:7

Proverbs
25:28

2 Timothy
1:7

Isaiah 26:3

Goodness Luke 18:18
Revelation 2:10
Meekness James 1:21

Colossians
3:12–13

Matthew 22:39

Philippians 4:7

Toward God
Goodness
Faithfulness
Meekness

Toward others
Love
Patience
Gentleness

Toward self
Joy
Peace
Self-control

Three Guards at the Perimeters

When I walk in a right relationship with God, I will produce the fruits of joy, peace and self-control. Automatically I will give love, patience and gentleness to others. I will honor God with goodness, faithfulness and meekness. Jesus said, "The thief comes only to steal and kill and destroy; I came that they may have life, and have it abundantly" (John 10:10). Satan desires to steal my joy, kill my peace and destroy my relationship with God.

Joy

The writer of Nehemiah wrote, "And do not be grieved, for the joy of the LORD is your strength" (Nehemiah 8:10). The joy of the Lord is our outer perimeter. It is our first defense against the enemy. Many Christians are joyless simply because the enemy was able to distract them from their focus on the Lord. When this happens, they become ineffective as Christians.

Satan often tries to steal our joy by using deceit. Someone says something fairly innocent, but when the words reach our ears they arrive twisted by Satan. We do not always hear correctly what was said. We begin to surmise and assume negative things instead of showing grace.

When we, because of a fiery dart, have lost our joy, we do not feel loving toward one another—and Satan stands on the sideline and laughs. We have forgotten who is our foe. This is spiritual warfare, and we do not even know that we are under fire because it starts so subtly!

95

Peace

If the enemy breaks through our perimeter of joy, he will attack the second perimeter and attempt to kill our peace. Isaiah writes, "Thou dost keep him in perfect peace, whose mind is stayed on thee, because he trusts in thee" (Isaiah 26:3). Satan will do whatever is possible to disrupt our peace and break our trust in God.

Peace is a fact of spiritual life for anyone who trusts the Lord. Terrorism cannot kill our peace. Trials and negative circumstances cannot kill our peace. Our peace is lost only when we focus on the negative circumstances facing us. Jesus said, "I have said this to you, that in me you may have peace . . ." (John 16:33). The word *may* indicates that peace is a choice. For every time we panic or become anxious, there was a peaceful, God-trusting choice we did not take. When we lose our focus on God, our peace leaves and we most certainly will not show patience toward one another.

Self-Control

If Satan has stolen my joy and killed my peace, it is because he wants to destroy my relationship with God. It also means that the enemy has gotten me so upset that I have lost my self-control. The writer of Proverbs says, "A man without self-control is like a city broken into and left without walls" (Proverbs 25:28). The pinnacle of success for Satan is when a Christian loses self-control. This means we are totally circumstance-centered, and he has unlimited opportunity to interfere in our relationship with God.

At this point, Satan has eliminated us as good Christian witnesses. When we become angry we will not show gentleness or grace. When we feel frightened, we will not respond with faith. When we are in difficulty, we will not stand firm in joy. Thoughts of God or of prayer do not enter our minds. Sin clogs the channel of communication. Isaiah writes, "But your iniquities have made a separation between you and your God, and your sins have hid his face from you so that he does not hear" (Isaiah 59:2).

I have heard many people say, "I was so angry I could not pray." That tells me that they had given the enemy permission to rent space in their heads. Our relationship with God gets temporarily put on hold when that happens. Not that we lose our salvation, but we lose our desire or ability to communicate with the Lord. The evil propaganda invasion has done its job.

How Satan Tries to Breach Our Perimeters

Satan's strategy depends on deceit and distraction in order to bring destruction. If we apply God's Word and strategy, we can defeat the enemy in spiritual warfare. Simply being aware of his intent to destroy relationships will bring victory in many spiritual battles.

Our enemy knows that if we become upset he can then provoke us to irritation and eventually anger. He also knows that when we are under stress we have a tendency to be easily upset. We are creatures of habit, and Satan uses that knowledge to his advantage when attacking our perimeters with his evil thoughts. Let's use criticism as an example of how Satan tries to use evil thoughts to steal our joy, kill our peace and destroy our relationships.

Let's say that you have had a wonderful day and seem to be on top of the world. You are very tired but looking forward to getting home and seeing your spouse. There is a picnic planned with the neighbors in your backyard, and you are filled with the joy of the Lord! At this point the enemy hates your positive attitude, so he grabs a bag of fiery darts.

Shortly after you arrive home, your spouse, having had a difficult day, says something that sounds awfully negative to you. Satan is shooting a flaming dart toward your mind, just as the boy threw a rock at the bear. Receiving the comment as criticism, you respond with a short, sharp reply to put your spouse down and justify yourself. The dart got past your shield. The evil propaganda has started!

The enemy is maneuvering your mind into a reactive, irritated position. He knows from your past that you can become defensive under stress, so he pours more negative thoughts into your mind as you mull over what your spouse said. Your flesh helps the enemy, of course, working overtime to justify the harsh things you said in reply. With all the noise going on inside, your chances of hearing God's voice get more and more slim.

Sometimes I think that Satan has two special-forces evil spirits, Bickering and Yelling, to help assault our perimeter of joy. Bickering specializes in supporting resistance cells and revolutionaries. He has a history of supporting our flesh, working through evil thoughts to rebel against the spirit. If Bickering takes control of a heart, a person would rather say many hateful, unholy things than lose an argument.

Yelling is a diversionary specialist—he is trained to distract. Yelling always speaks with a loud voice so that others cannot help but hear his side of the disagreement. His side is always a subtle diversion from the truth, and his objective is to prolong disagreements for as long as possible.

Bickering and Yelling together have wounded many souls. They are Satan's chief weapons in breaking through a perimeter of joy. Already wounded by a fiery dart, you continue to listen to their attack. Finally the outer perimeter of joy is completely breached by evil thoughts.

Sensing victory, Satan intensifies his attack on the second perimeter, with the intent to kill your peace. As he continues to rent space in your head, he enlarges the first critical comment in your mind. The enemy finally breaks through the second perimeter and you lose your peace. The principles of forgiveness are forgotten. You are becoming more irked with your spouse, so you launch another verbal attack, this one even stronger than the previous one.

You are fighting for the enemy and do not even know it! Satan shoots fiery darts like small gunfire into your thought patterns. By now you are getting ready for an all-out battle with your spouse, and the enemy has deflected your thinking from spiritual joy to working in the self-centered old nature. The evil propaganda is working!

Satan was able to steal your joy, kill your peace and now is targeting the third perimeter, which protects your relationship with God. As the fiery darts hit your mind, you become angry. Yelling accuses your spouse of something from the past—trying to put him or her on the defensive. It is a diversion intended to make your spouse back off so Bickering can win this confrontation. Satan has broken through the last perimeter and destroyed your self-control. Showing by your body action, tone of voice and glaring eyes, anger is now free to devour anyone in its way, just like a snarling tiger brought into captivity from the wild.

As you and your spouse continue to spar, you begin to focus some irritation and frustration on the children. Stung by the injustice of being civilian casualties, the children take their frustration out on each other, or on the dog. The dog chases the cat, and on and on it goes with everyone suffering.

The three perimeters have been breached. You are too angry to pray. Your relationships with your spouse and children are suffering. Now Satan wants to damage your relationship with God by bringing more evil thoughts to your mind.

Satan attacks your relationship with God by telling you that God really is not good. If God is good, why does He not stop the criticism by your spouse? Why did He not help you keep your good mood? If God is good, why does He not make your boss nicer, feed the hungry, stop the crime in your neighborhood and show more concern for His creation in general?

I have found that goodness is the nature and character of God. God's goodness gives expression to His love. Doctor Luke writes about the rich young ruler who addressed Jesus: "Good Teacher, what shall I do to inherit eternal life?" (Luke 18:18). Jesus responded by saying, "Why do you call me good? No one is good but God alone" (verse 19).

Satan desires to destroy any sign of God's goodness. If we can, in faith, hold on to that goodness, we will stand. Or sometimes, in His goodness, God's faithfulness holds on to us. The apostle Paul wrote, "If we are faithless, he remains faithful—for he cannot deny himself" (2 Timothy 2:13).

How to Guard the Perimeters

It is the responsibility of the Holy Spirit to alert us when we are coming under attack. If I am growing apathetic and taking God for granted, He calls me back to Himself. If I have been hurt by someone, He calls me to forgiveness.

I have discovered that to repulse the enemy from my perimeter of joy I must forgive those who hurt me. As soon as we forgive the one who has offended us, Satan withdraws and our joy returns. For years I have lived by an old axiom: "Never argue with a fool. No one watching can tell which one is the fool."

When two people are bickering and yelling in their self-centered old natures, they look ridiculous to those who do not want to hear and see the spectacle. The writer of Proverbs tells us, "A fool takes no pleasure in understanding, but only in expressing his opinion" (Proverbs 18:2). Disruption is Satan's way of making life an ongoing crisis. Paul writes to the Corinthians, "But all things should be done decently and in order" (1 Corinthians 14:40). Although this Scripture applies to church meetings, the principle covers all of life. God is a God of order.

If the enemy has overcome the perimeter of joy, he turns to attacking our peace. When the enemy attempts to kill our peace, God's mature soldiers call on the name of Jesus, the Prince of peace. Isaiah the prophet writes,

"In returning and rest you shall be saved; in quietness and in trust shall be your strength" (Isaiah 30:15).

Life is a mystery to be discovered and appreciated. We can gain spiritual wisdom and knowledge from everyday encounters. Through the Holy Spirit's training, I have realized that the best strategy for spiritual warfare is to set perimeters and let the Holy Spirit do the fighting. The evidence of joy, peace and self-control reveals that I am victorious.

6

FAITH

Facing the Unknown with Trust

After I completed my basic training in the United States, I was happy to be stationed in England for nine months. I had been trained as an aerial engineer and top-turret gunner in a B-17 bomber, so if any mechanical trouble occurred during flight, it was my job to repair the problem. We began to carry the air war to Germany.

April 8, 1944, began as so many English days begin—with clouds and a light mist. We were going on our seventh mission, this one to bomb a German airfield south of Hamburg. Excitement rose in me as we taxied down the tarmac toward takeoff. Minutes later we lifted off, and our airplane took its assigned place in the formation in the sky. The formation was like a V; each airplane had its place, just as in a flock of geese.

The clouds disappeared as we gained altitude, and the sky became clear over the English Channel. Looking at the water below, I was reminded of the many airmen who had landed their airplanes in its cold depths. Those planes had been so badly damaged by enemy gunfire that they could not fly back to England.

As we neared our target in Germany a pilot said, "Look at what's ahead." What he saw is called a box barrage. The enemy knew that we would have to go through a certain airspace to hit our target, and all the German antiaircraft guns in the region were aimed into this one section of airspace. As we entered the airspace, our B-17 bomber began to rock violently. We had gone through flak before, but never this bad. I was just hoping that none of the shells would hit our fuel tanks. I had seen several B-17s explode in midair from fuel tank hits.

The bomb bay doors were open as we entered the box barrage. With the tension of our situation, I was eager to hear and feel the bombs drop away. Finally, at the lead bombardier's command, I could see bombs descending from other bombers.

The pilot tried to close our bomb bay doors. They would not close. The controls had been shot to pieces. It was important that they be closed because open doors create an air drag that slows the airplane down and uses up too much fuel.

I left my top turret to crank the bay doors up manually by a handle located inside the bomb bay. To get to the handle I had to cross the bay on a catwalk. The catwalk was so narrow that I could not wear my parachute.

While I was attempting to crank up the bomb bay doors, I momentarily looked down at the ground 20,000 feet below and instantly wished I had not. If I were to get hit with even a small piece of the antiaircraft fire, I would probably fall all the way to the ground. Our engines were losing power. The controls were shot away on engine two. Number three was overheating. We were depending on engines one and four. The bomber was riddled with holes. Miraculously, none of the crew had been hit. We had just started flying over a large body of water, the *Zuider Zee*, when another engine died. The pilots saw that we could not make it to the other side, so they turned 180 degrees, bringing the airplane back over land. We were flying on one engine and losing altitude fast. The pilot gave the order to bail out. I was in the back of the B-17—and my parachute was in the front, across the catwalk and tucked into a tiny space near the top turret.

I made my way to my parachute and went to the back of the plane where there was more room to put it on. As I put it on, I glanced forward and saw the pilots jump out the bomb bay. The other crew members had already jumped. I had a choice: ride the plane down to where it would hit the ground and explode, or make my very first parachute jump.

As I looked at German-occupied Holland from an airplane door at seven thousand feet, I was aware that our plane was going to crash in enemy-held territory. The plane was flying near stall speed and going into a spin. I hesitated for a moment, weighing my options and my fears.

I was not a trained paratrooper, so if I was going to jump I had to trust whoever had packed my parachute.

I also had to depend on some silk cloth and a few ropes to somehow set me safely on the ground. I rolled forward out of the plane. The wind screamed at me, immediately tearing off my helmet. I hoped my parachute did not have flak holes in it.

Every airman who flew in the Air Force received at least one lesson on how to use a parachute. In my class the instructor explained the different principles that come into play when you are making a parachute jump.

With a chest-chute such as I had, it is best that the jumper be horizontal to the ground and facing up when the chute opens. If the jumper is in any other position there is danger of getting tangled in the cords on the parachute. If that happens the chute may fail to open or, when it does open, it may break bones or even strangle the jumper.

As I plummeted toward earth, I remembered what the instructor had said: "If you have the presence of mind, try some tricks such as rolling into a ball, or spread your legs and hands way apart and fly." I tried several positions as I was plunging earthward. They worked as he had said.

He had also said, "Free fall for as long as you can, because anyone caught dangling from a parachute is a target for German fighter pilots." I had a good long free fall, dropping below the three airmen who had jumped just before me.

When I pulled the rip cord, I was jerked suddenly to a halt as the parachute opened. My ears rang in the sudden silence. I felt as if I were in a vacuum or as if life had come to a standstill. Not for long. I looked down for what seemed a couple of seconds and watched our B-17 hit the side of a canal and explode in a ball of fire.

Suddenly the ground rushed up to meet my feet. I remembered to land on the balls of my feet, roll forward and pull the bottom reins of my parachute toward me. That helped force the air out of it so that it would collapse instead of dragging me along the ground. I landed as I had been taught. The instructor had done his job, and so had I.

Learning to Walk in Faith

As we grow up, we go to different schools—elementary, junior high, senior high and, for some, college and graduate school. For Christians there is also the school of the Holy Spirit. This school teaches the pupils how to walk in faith and about the weapons God uses in spiritual warfare.

God's nature is to accentuate the positive. When we face the unknown by faith and trust, we are telling God that we are intrigued by who He is and His creation. Consequently I have discovered that we absolutely cannot go where God's grace has not already gone! Faith cannot go ahead of grace, so we always have freedom, whether to fail or succeed.

The essence of faith and the qualities that give faith its identity are described by the writer of Hebrews: "Now faith is the assurance of things hoped for, the conviction of things not seen" (Hebrews 11:1). Faith has at its center two truths.

1. *The first truth of faith is "the assurance of things hoped for."* I used to think that the "things hoped for" were material things. Today, in this world of stress and perplexity, being in God's will is more and more the thing I hope for. By being in His will I can have assurance and wisdom to handle the problems of life.

Hope is based on the strength or goodness of someone else. A close relationship with God should be the number-one hope for all Christians. As Christians we can look ahead to an abundant life with God because He wants nothing but the best for us.

2. *The second truth of faith is the "conviction of things not seen."* If we could see life with the clarity of God's perspective, we would be astounded by the spiritual world that surrounds us. Then we would really get down to business with God. That is why faith faces the unknown—to bring into reality the unseen spiritual domain.

I believe that my life will always be a continuation of learning how to walk in faith. From the beginning God wanted me to learn the basic purpose of faith: to bring me into an intimate relationship with God the Father and Jesus Christ His Son. The apostle John writes, "And this is eternal life, that they know thee the only true God, and Jesus Christ whom thou hast sent" (John 17:3).

My simple description of *faith* is "acting upon God's call." Faith is active and progressive. God calls. I respond by obedience. God is glorified.

Faith starts and ends with God. The call from God is to seek and search for Him. Though faith starts with a call from God, the answer is within our spirit of adventure. Jesus promised, "Ask, and it will be given you; seek, and you will find; knock, and it will be opened to you" (Matthew 7:7). This means that our responses of faith complete a circle and result in intimate relationship with God.

I have discovered that the foundation stones of mature faith are focus, commitment and obedience. As I have struggled with the essence of faith, I have found that I need to focus on Christ. I learned that unless Christ comes first in my life I will be swept away by the circumstances of life.

As a new, excited Christian, I concluded that I needed spiritual experiences to confirm I was on the right track. Experiences with God moved my thinking from head knowledge to heart experience, always preparing me for a bolder step of faith. God gradually strengthened my faith, allowing me to go longer and longer between experiences—just trusting Him, based on His faithfulness. I now know that I cannot live by spiritual experiences, but it is still wonderful to see God's hand on my life, confirming His will by His manifest presence.

If faith culminates in an intimate relationship with God, where does faith start and how does faith face the unknown?

The Seed of Faith

My own walk of faith began when the Holy Spirit made me aware that there is a beginning, purpose and ending of life. Faith then became the vehicle for me to find God's answers about the season between the beginning and the end of my life. I was eager to know about God, but I was ignorant of faith that would reveal Him. My church had talked about the faith of the people in the Bible but gave me no examples of modern-day people of faith.

My breakthrough came when I read Ecclesiastes. Solomon writes:

I have seen the business that God has given to the sons of men to be busy with. He has made everything beautiful in its time; also he has put eternity into man's mind, yet so that he cannot find out what God has done from the beginning to the end.

Ecclesiastes 3:10–11

There was my starting point for faith: God has put eternity in every mind!

God gives us minds to seek, search and discover His will, yet our human minds are limited so we can never fully understand His plan. He has given us reasoning power, but not enough to unravel all the mysteries of life. Life then becomes the spiritual schoolhouse where we develop an intimate relationship with Him through faith.

I started contemplating what the Holy Spirit was saying to me in Ecclesiastes. God had given me a will to make proper or improper choices. Why? The simple answer is that it was His way of giving me the power to fulfill the God-given yearning for eternity within me. This spiritual yearning can only be filled by God. I reasoned that as I seek and search for God by faith, He will reveal His plan and purpose for my life.

An Unnamed Hunger

There is a spiritual vacuum inherent in every human. But the longing to fill that vacuum is dormant in the sinful human heart. We get so easily distracted. The longing must be nurtured, and then it will grow stronger, just as a muscle grows when exercised. This yearning desire from God tests the *principles* of life to find the *purpose* of life. Where did I come from? Why was I born? How can I live above the negative circumstances of life? Where will I go after I die?

Unless we find our true spiritual being, we are like an adopted child, restless until he finds his birth parents.

110

As Christians, we were adopted into God's family and will find out who we are only through Him.

The seed of yearning carries the potential of redeeming faith, growth in faith and service to God. This yearning is the starting, developing and driving force that either brings us closer to God or spends our energy on worldly pleasures. Out of this spiritual yearning comes a wrestling of the heart over who will be served—the fleshly desires of the self-centered old nature or God. This wrestling between good and evil takes place in every person's life. Hopefully it will take us into a walk of faith and a new name—"Christian."

This yearning for God, though misguided at times, has been revealed in history by people worshiping trees, mountains and the whole of creation. Idol worship can be seen in the stone faces on Easter Island or in Stonehenge, possibly created by the Druids of ancient England. They, along with the Israelites who worshiped the golden calf, were all involved in misguided faith.

Our modern-day idols are new cars, big homes, power, sex, food and freedom without responsibility. Too often these are the things that tell us who we are. We give them the power to say either "You are important," or "You are nothing special." We look to them for fulfillment but they consume us instead, and we remain hungry for the God of truth. The psalmist writes, "For all the gods of the peoples are idols; but the Lord made the heavens" (Psalm 96:5).

This is why it is extremely important that Christian parents bond with their children. A baby is not born with godly character. He or she is born with the sinful, self-centered old nature. A new baby immediately becomes the focus of everyone's attention. If his or her self-centered nature is indulged, the baby will be controlling all family activities in a very short time!

The baby needs to be born into a spiritual life. It is imperative that godly character be developed in the child to help fulfill his or her rightful destiny. What is taught early on will be revealed later in life. The teaching will have a direct bearing on whom the child serves: God or Satan.

Nurturing Faith

As the spiritual yearning in a child begins to mature, it is renamed "the spirit of adventure." The child begins to explore the physical world by checking out the pots and pans in the kitchen. The child constantly expands his or her exploration by learning to crawl, walk and then run.

If the child is confronted with *No! No!* when doing wrong and encouraged when doing something positive, he or she will begin to learn about boundaries and understand what is acceptable and what is not. As the spirits of adventure and conscience grow, the child quickly becomes responsible for choosing between right or wrong.

The line between self will and God's will is called the line of discretion. *Discretion* means "carefulness in what we say or do." We are confronted many times a day by the line of discretion; always we have to make a choice. We must choose between serving God and our conscience and serving our sinful, self-centered old nature and the powers of darkness. Choosing self always looks safe, practical and sensible to our old nature. But the spirit of adventure, led by the Holy Spirit, is willing to throw everything away in exchange for the love and plan of God.

The following diagram shows how this works:

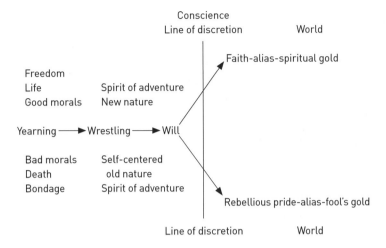

If the spirit of adventure is nurtured, it will begin to cross the line of discretion into God's will, where it receives a new name: Faith! Each time we cross over the line of discretion in faith, our lives submit more fully to God and to the blessings of His approval.

Maturing Faith

Often God is testing us to see if we want to walk the road that Jesus trod. As Jesus trusted in His Father, we, too, must learn how to enter that arena of trust and let the Holy Spirit work out our salvation. This is when the spirit of adventure may be released into a deeper spiritual dimension! Crossing the line of discretion in faith, we experience many powerful blessings as we learn the way of the cross.

113

If the spirit of adventure is not continually sanctified by the work of the Holy Spirit, we will be tempted instead by the powers of darkness. But Satan's tempting is futile if we recognize the attack and determine to trust God and stay away from temptation. This is why spiritual yearning and the spirit of adventure need godly instruction at an early age—so that they do not take life for granted. Taking life for granted causes traditionalism and brings death to the spirit of adventure. A lack of teaching, understanding or daring faith will keep our spiritual lives at a standstill.

For some people the fear of changing old habits is too big to overcome. As a result, they live in bondage to their self-centered old natures. Their spirits cannot find a living, growing spiritual expression in life. As the spirit of adventure combines with our self-centered old natures, it is renamed "Rebellious Pride," which has an alias: "Fool's Gold."

Fool's Gold is a false faith that brings attention and applause to itself. It seems good, but it works hard to steal glory from God. The major goal of Rebellious Pride is to accommodate and satisfy the self-centered old nature.

I believe that we see Fool's Gold in action as mankind climbs the highest mountains, dives deep in the oceans and drives the fastest cars. It is always taunting the unknown, playing near the line called death—sometimes crossing over. It is easy to see where Rebellious Pride has been because of the devastation left behind. It performs great feats, but only for its own fame. It often uses deceit, duplicity and distortion as tools, and they are dangerous tools. Once a person gets accustomed to them, they are hard to put down.

The spirit of Rebellious Pride has led to many an adulterous affair. Riots, gossip and school shootings are all the products of a spirit of adventure that has been corrupted by Satan. They are the results of spiritual warfare.

King Saul was a powerful king who was overtaken by Rebellious Pride. God, through Samuel the prophet, told King Saul to destroy every person in the Amalekite nation. Instead, Saul spared their leader, King Agag. He also allowed his people to plunder the spoils of war—in direct disobedience to the Lord, who had said to destroy even the treasure.

The voices and praises of his people had become more important to Saul than the voice of God. God had given King Saul victory over the Amalekites, but Saul crossed the line of discretion by his rebellious pride, and because of his disobedience lost his kingship. The author of 1 Samuel writes, "For rebellion is as the sin of divination, and stubbornness is as iniquity and idolatry" (1 Samuel 15:23).

Why does God require His people to have faith? The apostle John writes, "For whatever is born of God overcomes the world; and this is the victory that overcomes the world, our faith" (1 John 5:4).

Battlefield Faith

My response to faith changed my life in 1969, a year after my son Rick's death. I went to work as usual but could not shake the sudden thought that I was supposed to sell my business. I had ten to twenty employees and sold rebuilt automotive parts in the upper Midwest. Was selling the business that I enjoyed on God's mind?

I knew that something spiritual was happening to me, but I was not sure what. For months our church bulletin had carried a motto, "To Love Is to Care Is to Act." Was the Holy Spirit speaking for me to act?

Two heads are generally better than one, so I called my wife to ask her what she thought. She suggested we pray over the phone. She asked God for a sign that the business should be sold right away.

By the time I went home that night, I had committed to sell. I made no telephone calls, told no one that I was ready to sell, but God answered our prayer. Within two weeks a deal was consummated, and I was out of the business.

Christ was the reason for this dramatic step, and faith became the vehicle to take me into the next stage of spiritual growth. It was not a mid-life crisis but a spiritual adventure. Something better was ahead for me. I did not know what it was, but I knew that in due time faith would disclose it. I was ready to face the unknown because faith can see only success!

I became more excited about this adventure as I understood that the faith I was learning would always be essential to my spiritual walk. God had a new life for me, but I had to receive it by letting go of the past and launching out into the unknown future.

How Faith Is Revealed

My wife and I were beginning to experience life in a whole new way. People were coming to us for counseling about their relationships. We regularly prayed for people to be healed and for a variety of other needs. I began to understand that faith reveals itself in at least four ways. It brought God recognition and made me aware of His glory!

1. *Faith recognizes God.* The purpose of faith is to reveal God so we can believe in all that He is. Faith, then, becomes the key that opens our hearts to spiritual maturity and warfare. The writer to the Hebrews declares, "And without faith it is impossible to please him. For whoever would draw near to God must believe that he exists and that he rewards those who seek him" (Hebrews 11:6).

I was sitting in my favorite chair at home, reflecting on how much I had grown spiritually. Like Job, I was holding onto my righteousness and patting myself on my back. The Holy Spirit broke into my mind and reminded me of who is in charge by asking two questions: *Who gives you the next breath? Who gives you the next heartbeat?*

I quickly responded, *You do!*

I saw then that understanding the fullness of God comes by illumination to my soul. I knew that God reveals Himself through His creation, but He was a figment of my intellectual imagination until I experienced His reality. This revelation—that God must illuminate my spirit in order for me to receive truth—taught me to appreciate my own salvation. Through this new appreciation of faith I was being prepared for more understanding.

I realized that I can never hope to please God unless He first reaches down to me. Through my obedience to His illumination (call it *faith*), God would be glorified in me. Faith then would teach me how to walk through the process of sanctification. The apostle Paul writes, "And we all, with unveiled face, beholding the glory of the Lord, are being changed into his likeness from one degree of glory to another; for this comes from the Lord who is the Spirit" (2 Corinthians 3:18).

The apostle Paul gained a new understanding of God while on the road to Damascus. He was persecuting Christians at the time but thought that he was serving God. Paul was confronted by the Light (Jesus) on the road to Damascus, and he responded with faith by obeying and serving Jesus as his Messiah. He realized that the only way for him was total involvement with Christ. From that time forth he chose to abandon his traditionalism and invested everything that he had in Christ. He no longer saw Jesus Christ as his opponent, but as his Commander-in-Chief!

Paul's newfound faith propelled him into a spiritual ministry of building up rather than destroying. Paul discovered that if he freed his faith to obey God, his faith would free him to live.

2. *Faith changes me.* After I had sold my business, I asked the Lord for June and July off to contemplate the change. I knew that, following those two months, I would need work. God was faithful. On the first day of August, two months to the day, Pastor Roy Hendrickson called me.

Pastor Hendrickson was the director of a ministry to college youth called Lutheran Youth Encounter (LYE). The gist of our conversation was that LYE had no money but needed a business manager.

Lutheran Youth Encounter was an organization that had singing and witnessing teams at various colleges. These teams took the Gospel to other college campuses and churches to challenge young people to receive Christ. This was the same type of team that had challenged my son Rick to receive Christ. That interaction had changed his life. Maybe I was being challenged? I told Pastor Hendrickson that I would like to pray, then call him back.

I was not positive that LYE was the place I should be. I wanted to make sure that I heard from God. After a short time in prayer, I was impressed that *This is where I can at least start on my spiritual journey.*

It was a whole new step of faith for me. I had to learn how to listen to others and consider their thoughts and concerns. I was no longer the one who made the final decisions. This became a bold new step in faith. It was not easy, and life can be a tough teacher, but I was determined to follow God's will as best I understood it. God did not want me to continue on a worldly path but desired to show me a better way.

3. *Faith grows.* God wanted to train me in a deeper walk of faith. He did that through Dr. Herbert Mjorud and Pastor Morris Vaagenes. Dr. Mjorud invited Pastor Vaagenes to travel with him on a ministry trip to the Far East. Pastor Vaagenes, having the hunger of an evangelist for reaching lost souls, immediately said yes. He did have some reservations: He would be leaving his family and his work and the ministry at North Heights Lutheran where charismatic renewal was beginning to blossom. Whom would he leave in charge?

I was his pastoral assistant, though I was not ordained. Because I came from a successful business background and showed some signs of spiritual leadership, Pastor Vaagenes considered asking me.

After much prayer, he asked me if I would be responsible for leadership in the congregation while he was on the crusade. The Holy Spirit had recently quickened my spirit when I read in Isaiah, "Enlarge the place of your tent, and let the curtains of your habitations be stretched out; hold not back, lengthen your cords and strengthen your stakes" (Isaiah 54:2) so my immediate response was also yes. Intuitively in my spirit, I knew that God wanted me to take another step toward spiritual maturity. I was given permission by Pastor Vaagenes and the church board to conduct all services, including Lenten services, which were to start that Wednesday evening. God was preparing me for a step in growing faith.

I am an advocate of the priesthood of all believers, as laid down in the New Testament. I immediately began to involve "lay people" in all aspects of our church services. What transpired in the two and a half months Pastor Vaagenes was absent became a big part of breaking down our church's traditional mentality—one that said laity cannot do spiritual ministry.

The congregation and I grew in faith during that time. As we sought God for His leadership there came a maturing, trust and confidence that He would lead us on our pilgrimage of faith. Faith became a vehicle, love the cargo!

I was challenged by God to face the spiritual unknown. It was the process of sanctification by which I learned in a greater way how to discern and how to exercise my will to choose His way.

Growing faith is the result of seeking and searching for answers to the mysteries of life. The apostle Paul writes to the Thessalonians, "We are bound to give thanks to God always for you, brethren, as is fitting, because your faith is growing abundantly, and the love of every one of you for one another is increasing" (2 Thessalonians 1:3).

Faith is nourished when we choose to follow the leading of the Holy Spirit. Active faith is confirmed by the love we experience for one another. If we cannot love and accept each other as we are, we are not growing in faith. Our faith in the spiritual is proved by God's love being released in our lives.

Bible study, seminars and fellowship groups became special times for me. As the Holy Spirit began to change my worldly thought patterns, I discovered that spiritual truth is given on the mountaintop, and that the mountaintop experiences are preparation for life in the valley. The mental understanding we gain on the mountaintop becomes heart-truth in the valley of life, as we by faith explore the unknown.

4. *Faith is needed for spiritual warfare.* In 1976 I was in the Twin Cities at a meeting of charismatic leaders from around the country. Several of the leaders had met earlier to set up the agenda, and they believed that this meeting had been called by the Lord. We all arrived with the expectation that the Holy Spirit would show us the next step in charismatic renewal.

With the joyous arrival of all participants, the meeting was soon underway. The agenda began to unfold early in the meeting, and it was not long before I began to feel uneasy. There was a "hidden agenda" that was subtly being disclosed.

Several men were trying to bring a change in leadership. They had not previously informed the present leadership of this desire for change, and I felt that this was a coup. I did not believe that what was happening was of God.

My spirit began to grieve deeply. Several times I fought within myself to keep from leaving the meeting. Since the meeting seemed to reach no agreement, we broke up early to retire for the evening. Spiritual warfare was going on!

After visiting for a little while I went to bed, hoping everything would fade away overnight. Not able to sleep because of my grieving spirit, I arose and went for a drive in my prayer chariot—my car. I needed to get alone with the Lord and try to get a clear answer for why my mind was upset and my spirit was unsettled.

I drove to a restaurant seventy miles north of the Twin Cities and had breakfast at two in the morning. After breakfast I decided to drive to my cabin, where the Holy Spirit had spoken to me countless times. It was a place of God's presence and peace. As I parked alongside the cabin, I noticed the beauty of being in the dark alone with the Lord.

I began praying in tongues, letting the Spirit inside me articulate feelings that I could not put words to. Suddenly the inside of my car filled with a soft light, although it was still dark outside. It was so light that I could have read a newspaper. As fast as the light came, so did waves of peace. I knew in my spirit that I could rest, because the problem was in God's hands.

Driving back to the meeting in the morning was easy, because my burden had been lifted. Sure enough, the dissenting men realized during the morning meeting that they could not come to an agreement, and the hidden agenda was dropped. This was the result of spiritual warfare!

Sometimes God allows things to happen that are not in agreement with His will but do reveal His perfect love. God knows that in a tough spiritual battle, growing faith will eventually bring a positive conclusion.

Just as Satan attacked Jesus, he will also attack us when we stand up for Jesus. Satan knows when we lapse into worldly thinking, and if we do not recognize that we have, he takes advantage of us.

The apostle Paul writes,

> No, in all these things we are more than conquerors through him who loved us. For I am sure that neither death, nor life, nor angels, nor principalities, nor things present, nor things to come, nor powers, nor height, nor depth, nor anything else in all creation, will be able to separate us from the love of God in Christ Jesus our Lord.
>
> Romans 8:37–39

With this assurance we can walk confidently in victory, knowing that God upholds us in all circumstances of life. This guarantee gives us an inward awareness of Christ, allowing others to see Christ in our outward appearances!

As God's soldiers, we need to use our spiritual vision to probe the powers of darkness. Probing calls for faith to overcome the fears, deceit, lies and half-truths. We must be able to look through the shrouding mist and see the truth God has for us.

Fear stands on the sideline of life, too preoccupied with itself to face the unknown, and robbing the fearful person of his spiritual heritage. Fear and unbelief constantly wait for an opportunity to pounce and steal the godly joy that is found in released faith. That is spiritual warfare!

Faith, working hand in hand with trust, looks into the future, always taking the best course for our well-being. As Pastor George Voeks said, "Living in faith is learning to walk at the brink of disaster, knowing that God holds the safety net."

Faith not only brings lost souls to salvation but is an instrument of the Holy Spirit to take us through the uncharted territory of life to spiritual maturity. The primary purpose of faith is to bring God's people into an intimate relationship with Him. When our yearnings and spirits of adventure turn into faith, we can look into the spiritual world and see God. Once we see Him, we recognize that we are involved in the spiritual warfare between heaven and the powers of darkness.

Then faith, powered by the Holy Spirit, reveals God's strategy over the powers of darkness! For the mature Christian, life is nothing more than faith in action.

7

BATTLEFIELD COMMUNICATIONS

After parachuting into hostile, enemy-held territory, I looked up at the B-17 bombers flying back to England and experienced a horrible feeling of being alone and abandoned. Questions came to my mind: *What will happen now? Will I be captured? Will I be killed in German-occupied Holland?* I had lost all communication with my friends.

Suddenly the two pilots and radio operator who had parachuted from our stricken bomber came running up to me. We had a joyous reunion despite our difficult situation. It was good to have someone else to communicate with as we contemplated the intense new challenge that confronted us.

None of us knew how to speak either German or Dutch. Even if we could have spoken a few words in the native languages, it would have been with an American accent. We knew that it was only a matter of time before we would have to talk to strangers. How would we communicate?

I felt much the same way when God began calling me to interact with the spiritual world. I was a stranger. What was I supposed to say? What was I supposed to do? I had some head knowledge but no real understanding in my heart. The Air Force had taught me how to do battle in the physical world. Now the Holy Spirit wanted to teach me battlefield communications in the unseen world.

Basics of Battlefield Communication

As a recruit in the spiritual realm, I discovered that I could make my life easier by learning how to converse with God. Eventually I found that interaction with Him is just communicating what is on my mind.

Soon after I began to learn about prayer, I was confronted with a problem: The powers of darkness will do whatever is necessary to keep me from getting the word for my life from my Commander.

I sincerely wanted a quiet time with God. But as I began to pray, disturbing thoughts would come to my mind. I remembered that I needed to clean the garage, cut the grass or do any number of chores that would prevent me from interacting with God.

My problematic habit of getting ambushed was dealt with after I met a retired evangelist, a friend of Lutheran Youth Encounter. He had such a powerful spiritual experience that some people thought he had gone over the mental edge and had lost his ability to think rationally. He did, in fact, end up in an institution for a period of time. He carried with him a reminder of his spiritual experience: Both of his hands had deep indentations, like scarred-over nail wounds.

On one visit I asked him about prayer. He said, "Always be aware of the presence of God. Regardless of where you are or the circumstance you are facing, remember that the Holy Spirit is dwelling in you. Prayer is a conversation with God, just as you would speak to a friend. Talking with the Lord should be as natural as breathing. Each breath and heartbeat should be praise, for it is a gift of grace. The time and place to pray is always right now, right here!"

He also spoke about a clean heart. "I have had many people ask why God does not answer their prayers. There can be a variety of reasons, but the basic reason is often that sin is hindering the prayer. It is important that we start with a clean heart. Just as we would not want to drink out of a dirty cup or glass, it is important that sin not dirty our communion with God."

Isaiah the prophet writes,

Behold, the Lord's hand is not shortened, that it cannot save, or his ear dull, that it cannot hear; but your iniquities have made a separation between you and your God, and your sins have hid his face from you so that he does not hear.

Isaiah 59:1–2

This does not mean that we can lose our salvation, but that our communication channel with God can be clogged.

127

I told my friend, "I ask forgiveness for stupid things I do as I go through the day, and confess my sins of omission, those things I know I should do but fail to do."

He agreed with me. "It is relatively easy to confess the sins of thought, word and deed, but we generally want the sin of omission to take a back seat as if it does not matter. It does! The apostle John said, 'If we confess our sins, he is faithful and just, and will forgive our sins and cleanse us from all unrighteousness'" (1 John 1:9).

He went on to say, "Most people tell God what they want, and then turn away, as if He has left to run their errand. They treat Him like a bellhop. If they would wait and listen to what comes into their thoughts, they would hear His answer. Sometimes the answer comes right away, and sometimes we have to wait. God does not answer according to our time schedule, but in the fullness of His time!

"When we place our heads on our pillows at night, we should say, 'In Jesus' name, Amen.' In other words, we should have been in continual awareness of God's presence, listening and conversing with Him throughout the day. Conversation with God is the way we open our hearts to hear His answers!"

I began to get excited as the understanding of God's truth started to break through my preconceived idea of prayer. From that time I was free to talk to God on a more personal basis. God was not "out there somewhere," but He was within me!

Soon after our discussion a man came to me, deeply troubled about prayer. He said, "Prayer is one of the hardest things for me to do because I am so busy. It is difficult to find time to spend on my knees and just focus on God. Surveys show that most pastors spend just a few minutes in prayer and devotions. If they, as God's leaders, do not find time to pray, how can I, a layman, be expected to find time?"

I replied, "Life is filled with choices. We all have the same amount of time; what we do with the time reveals our priorities. Yes, there are times when it is desirable to be quiet and alone with the Lord, but we can also pray in the busy times—in the midst of life.

"No matter where we are, we can still be God-conscious and talk to God, either in our learned language or in transcendent tongues. God is eager to hear what we are thinking. God already knows our needs, but He longs for us to recognize our needs and voice them to Him."

The Christian way is not easy. It is not the walk of the fainthearted, but the way of the committed. I have concluded that there are three stages to growing in prayer.

Stage 1: Spiritual Recruit

When I first started to pray, it was an expression of my human thoughts toward God. As I conversed with God, I gradually began to think God's thoughts, because He has a better way for my life than my sinful mind could produce.

I began to understand that praying is an act of my will. There were times I did not feel like praying, but if I started to pray my feelings soon lined up with my prayer.

Looking back I see that, as a prayer recruit, my desires were often myopic. My thoughts urged me to ask for whatever was close to my heart, especially in the personal, family and material arenas. Going to God for my needs was like going to the local grocery or department store. God became a warehouse stocked with goodies—a doting Father.

I learned that God is not too busy to answer my little problems. It seemed as if He answered while I was still asking. When I asked for smaller needs and saw them answered, they became faith-builders for bigger requests. Paul writes to the Philippians, "But in everything by prayer and supplication with thanksgiving let your requests be made known to God" (Philippians 4:6).

God is not too busy to take care of small things like colds, sore throats and parking places.

As recruits, one of the first prayers we learn is the Lord's Prayer. Several men were talking about this prayer at a breakfast recently, and a young man asked me, "What do you think most people get from the Lord's Prayer?"

I responded, "I do not know what others receive from saying the prayer, but I know what I get! When I pray 'Our Father,' my mind goes to who is in charge. When I pray 'Thy Kingdom come,' my mind connects to what Paul writes to the Romans, 'For the kingdom of God is not food and drink but righteousness and peace and joy in the Holy Spirit.'

"I used to pray the Lord's Prayer out of ritualism, unaware that this prayer is part of spiritual warfare. When I prayed 'Thy Kingdom come' I did not even know what God's Kingdom consisted of; I was more concerned about 'Forgive us our trespasses.' Now as I walk in an ongoing awareness of forgiveness, my emphasis is on God's Kingdom coming with righteousness, peace and joy in the Holy Spirit. Our resting in the righteousness of Jesus brings peace, which is expressed in spiritual joy."

The young man thanked me and declared, "I have never known that I was praying for God's Kingdom of righteousness, peace and joy. I did not realize that the enemy wants to keep peace and joy out of my life!" He had begun to understand that prayer encompasses far more than simple duty.

Prayer is a starting place for spiritual recruits, but it is certainly not the place to stop. My young friend was being prepared for the next stage: becoming a warrior in the battlefield.

Stage 2: Warrior in Battle

The words "prayer warrior" remind me of Pastor Fred Herzog, a powerful man of God. My wife and I once took about fifty young people to a charismatic meeting he was leading. After singing and teaching, Pastor Fred turned to the group's prayer needs. I was new in the Holy Spirit and eager to be involved.

Pastor Fred asked me to pray with him for a young man who had curvature of the spine. As the bent-over young man stood up, I noticed how difficult it was for him to walk. I thought to myself that the Holy Spirit had a big job on His hands.

I stood up and closed my eyes as we laid hands on the young man. When Pastor Fred started to pray my hands began to tremble, as if I was dragging a heavy chain across a sharp edge. This young man's body was shaking violently, an indication that his body was changing. After Pastor Fred finished praying, I added a few words, then opened my eyes.

The young man's posture had changed. He was taller than before we prayed!

The other young people broke out in praise for his healing. They had grown up with this young man and were aware of his affliction. I had learned that healing was God's job; mine was to be obedient and pray.

My wife and I were awakened early one morning. A strong wind from the west was blowing the drapes in the bedroom almost straight away from the window. As we awakened, my wife asked me to close the windows while she closed them in other rooms. It was springtime and she anticipated a rainstorm.

Reentering the bedroom she said, "I noticed the sky is clear and the moon is reflecting off the still pond. Why were the drapes windblown while it is quiet otherwise?"

Suddenly we knew why. We both had a deep concern for the soldiers fighting in Vietnam. We knew someone was in great danger of being killed or wounded, but we did not know who. The call to prayer was not for our son, because he had already died. Suddenly into our minds came the name "Marcus."

We knelt immediately alongside the bed and began praying in tongues, sobbing occasionally as the Spirit led. The anguish we had experienced for our son returned to us with force as we cried out for Marcus' life. Who better to call to God with prayer than parents who had lost their own son in the same circumstances? We persisted in prayer for about an hour. Suddenly the burden was lifted—as if a heavy weight had been taken off our hearts. There seemed to be a holy hush, confirmed by peace. We went back to sleep, very tired from the event.

One week later I mentioned this odd night to some co-workers. One of the men got a strange look on his face and said, "I have just heard from my son, Marcus.

He was out on patrol that night and was involved in a firefight with the enemy. Most of his patrol was killed, but my son was spared."

I have learned to pray for the same subject until I receive a release in my spirit. To be released by the Holy Spirit means that an inner peace assures me that what He purposed has been accomplished.

Persistence in prayer is one of the strengths of prayer warriors. Many people say that to repeat the same prayer is a lack of faith. According to this theory, we would pray only once for our family, as more prayer would demonstrate a lack of faith. I do not believe that.

Jesus was persistent as He prayed the following prayer three times: "My Father, if it be possible, let this cup pass from me; nevertheless, not as I will, but as thou wilt" (Matthew 26:39).

It is important that we pray until we are released from the concern. Jesus said,

"Which of you who has a friend will go to him at midnight and say to him, 'Friend, lend me three loaves; for a friend of mine has arrived on a journey, and I have nothing to set before him'; and he will answer from within, 'Do not bother me; the door is now shut, and my children are with me in bed; I cannot get up and give you anything'? I tell you, though he will not get up and give him anything because he is his friend, yet because of his importunity he will rise and give him whatever he needs."

Luke 11:5–8

As I learned how to be a warrior on the spiritual battlefield, the Holy Spirit taught me persistence, because He wanted to teach me about a new phase of prayer—*intercession.*

Stage 3: Intercessor

I have visited many different churches as a guest speaker, and the call to intercession over these places has come many times. God once revealed to me the spiritual poverty of a church in northern Minnesota. As I was praying in tongues, the Holy Spirit began to form a picture in my mind. He took me inside the church through a walkout basement door, and I saw that the downstairs was filled with mummies.

Then the Spirit took me upstairs into the sanctuary where the pews were filled with mummies. These mummies were bodies wrapped with cloth, as Lazarus was before Jesus called him out of the tomb (see John 11:43). God wanted to do a spiritual resurrection and, just as Jesus told the spectators to unbind Lazarus, Betty and I were there to unbind the congregation from their negative attitudes in the church.

The Holy Spirit spoke to my mind and said, *They are bound with unforgiveness, wrong priorities and an unwillingness to let Me be God. My people are more spiritually dead than alive. I weep for them as they live for themselves. They are not concerned about their relationships and do not have My heartache and concern for the lost souls in this area.*

At these words, I broke out in deep sobbing and prayer. The Lord had given me His heart for the people. What else could I do?

Later, while Betty and I were having lunch at an elder's house, he asked, "How do you think God sees our church?" Since he had asked, I shared with him the vision the Holy Spirit had revealed to me. He, his wife, my wife and I began together to weep deeply. The four of us were filled with a deep sighing as God shared His heart and concern.

At times God raises up intercessors to pray His people through difficult circumstances that they could not handle by themselves. The writer of Isaiah tells about Jesus, "He bore the sin of many, and made intercession for the transgressors" (Isaiah 53:12).

Paul writes to the Romans, "Likewise the Spirit helps us in our weakness; for we do not know how to pray as we ought, but the Spirit himself intercedes for us with sighs too deep for words" (Romans 8:26).

In intercession I see from God's perspective what needs to be changed. I must be ready to confess any sin I might see in the intercession. Intercessory prayer is seeing and experiencing heartache from the Lord's perspective and entering vicariously to voice God's concern.

Holy Spirit Empathy

I was asked to speak for several days at a well-established church down south. The pastor and his wife were powerful leaders in charismatic renewal, and the church was well-known all over the world.

The church was experiencing some frustration. They had stopped growing spiritually and numerically. They had come to a stalemate in most of their relationships. There was not the closeness that they had experienced previously as a growing church family.

My wife and I were staying at the pastor's home, and on Sunday afternoon I excused myself to seek the Holy Spirit's message for the evening service. I went into the bedroom for some quiet time.

As I was seeking the message, these words came suddenly to my mind, *You have prospered and become smug in your richness.* After the words came, I collapsed on the floor. I could hear my heart beating in my ears. I could feel God's grief. What I was experiencing was overwhelming.

Deep out of the depths of my being came groans, followed by sobbing. My body convulsed and shook as the sobbing continued. I could not help being a little noisy. My spirit was groaning. The words *You have prospered and become smug in your richness* kept going through my mind.

Everything subsided after several minutes, and waves of peace flooded my body. My mind began to fill with thoughts that the Holy Spirit wanted me to speak at the evening meeting. The Holy Spirit had given me the topic, and now He was giving me the message.

As the four of us gathered around the dinner table for a light snack, the pastor asked, "What is the message for tonight?" I was not eager to tell, but I was a guest in his home, so I shared what had happened. It was an extremely difficult time for him because he was confronted with the church's bondage.

I was uncomfortable. No one likes to be God's messenger of rebuke! So I tried that evening to preach a message different from what the Holy Spirit had given me. When I concluded that message, the pastor asked me to tell what the Holy Spirit had said that afternoon.

I did not want to, but I obeyed. As soon as I began to speak the Spirit's message, many people left their chairs and prostrated themselves on the floor! I repeated the message of "You have prospered and become smug in your richness" several times. After delivering the Holy Spirit's message, I collapsed at the altar and began to sob. The Holy Spirit was still interceding.

There was crying, sobbing and wailing all over the church as the Holy Spirit brought conviction. He was doing a restoration work! The apostle Peter said, "Repent therefore, and turn again, that your sins may be blotted out, that times of refreshing may come from the presence of the Lord" (Acts 3:19). The Lord was bringing both repentance and refreshing that night.

During the meeting, four church elders were in another place praying about the stalemate in the church. The Holy Spirit confirmed the word He had given me by telling them that their church had become smug and prosperous.

The pride that had sneaked into their fellowship was revealed by the Holy Spirit and kicked out through repentance! The Holy Spirit interceded, bringing the truth of God against the church's waywardness. That was spiritual warfare!

Praying in Tongues

My prayer life really changed when I was baptized in the Holy Spirit and began to speak in a strange tongue. The basic purpose for speaking in tongues is to pray according to God's will. As I speak in tongues, I become more aware of God's presence. The spirit within me communicates straight to God what is on my heart. When I do not know how to pray, I speak out in tongues, praying exactly what is in my spirit. There is no room for confusion, being double-minded or in error.

The prayer language of tongues is one of the ways I pray daily. Tongues are a Holy Spirit gift directed toward God. The spirit within a person prays without interference by the conscious mind. It is perfect communication between my spirit and the Holy Spirit. It is battlefield communication that Satan cannot corrupt.

I found that one of the most difficult things to remove from prayer was my human desires. The gift of tongues bypasses my mind, making the prayer pure and not motivated by the desires of my mind. Self is set aside. This is why tongues are an enigma to my mind; my mind cannot control tongues.

Some people choose not to speak in tongues. I believe that many do not desire to speak in tongues because they lack either understanding of the gift, faith or humility. Their choice does not invalidate the gift for those who accept it.

"He Knows My Need"

Several years ago I was involved in a number of regional clergy seminars. The seminars were attended by area pastors and their spouses, with about forty people at each meeting.

On one occasion my wife and I attended a regional church seminar in southern Wisconsin, where Pastor Larry Christenson had a Bible study concerning the works of the Holy Spirit. After the study, we spent time in prayer, trying to hear and discern what the Holy Spirit would continue to say.

Finally the silence was broken by a woman who started to cry softly. With an emotion-filled voice, she asked if she could have prayer for the baptism of the Holy Spirit. Four of us immediately laid hands on her and prayed for the filling of the Holy Spirit.

As we prayed, she suddenly burst forth speaking in a new language, the gift of tongues. Several others asked for the baptism, and the Holy Spirit graciously moved so that whoever asked for the infilling received it.

One pastor delivered a prophetic message from God, and then others joined with prophecies speaking to personal and congregational needs. It was a joyous and powerful time in the presence of the Holy Spirit! Some people say the gifts of the Holy Spirit are not for today. But the Holy Spirit was revealing Himself in an obvious way to strengthen, challenge, encourage and validate God's leaders.

Before the meeting two women, both pastors' wives, had decided that they would take a break from the seminar and go shopping in a large town nearby. Absent from the meeting, they missed being part of what many had experienced.

When they saw my wife before dinner at the church, both of them asked, "We heard what happened. Will you pray for us at the church altar rail?"

Betty quickly replied, "Let me get my husband!" Finding me visiting with several pastors, she quietly said, "Two pastors' wives want prayer. Will you pray with us?"

We met the women at the altar rail. Kneeling inside the altar rail, I asked the first woman, "What can the Lord do for you?" She told me what was on her heart. It was easy to pray for her need.

The second woman replied, "God knows my need." Again, bowing my head, I softly prayed in tongues, then waited on the Lord to give understanding and meet her needs. Suddenly an image appeared in my mind—a small woven basket filled with violets, and an egg standing on end in the middle.

When I shared what I saw, she broke out sobbing. After she gained her composure she said, "He knew my need! The last thing my young son gave me before being accidentally killed was a small basket filled with violets and one egg upright in the middle!"

She was reassured and challenged to another level of spiritual growth as God revealed through the gifts of the Holy Spirit that He was very much aware of her need. She and her friend left the altar with a new understanding of the depth of God's love. I came away with the expectation that God wanted to teach me something new.

Something new was not long in coming. As a pastoral assistant, I made many hospital calls. One of my next visits was with a man who had suffered a stroke. When I entered his hospital room, he was lying on the bed face-up. He looked as if he was in a trance with both eyes wide open. He was unable to communicate or respond to my greeting.

Standing by his bed I greeted him again, but there was absolutely no response from him. I asked the Lord out loud if it was possible to communicate with the man through the Holy Spirit. A thought entered my mind that I should ask the man, "If you can hear me, give me a sign."

He responded by blinking just his right eye, three times! It seemed obvious to me that, in his spirit, he had heard me.

At that instant I understood how the spirit of a person can be praying at all times, even if the mind is not functioning as it should. If the spirit within is praying without ceasing, the Alzheimer's unit in a nursing home could be God's prayer palace!

We are all busy, but we are given equal amounts of time: 24 hours a day. If we are willing to take time for a conversation with God, He will bless us beyond our capacity to understand. I am not talking about material blessings, but about self-acceptance, peace and the guidance we need for our lives.

Battlefield conversation is a frontline, offensive weapon in spiritual warfare. Our well-being and the fullness of abundant life hinge on our conversations with God. What we pray or do not pray as a recruit, warrior or intercessor determines the outcome of our spiritual battles.

When we talk to our Commander, we can do so with confidence that He hears us. God calls all Christians to converse with Him that we might fight in spiritual warfare, unified in the Holy Spirit! Learning how to pray prepared me for discerning enemy tactics in spiritual warfare.

8

GOD'S UNDERGROUND

Discerning Enemy Tactics

After four of my crew from the shot-down bomber regrouped on the ground, we had to agree on a course of action. We were in German-held territory and did not want to become prisoners of war. After some discussion, we decided to go south, hoping we would meet the Dutch underground movement. We believed they would help us get to Spain and eventually to England.

Going south, we were confronted by a large canal. Looking to our left we saw a boat and three men sitting about a mile from us, near the best crossing. There were three of them, but four of us, so we decided to try to take the boat so we could cross the canal.

As we approached the three men, one shouted to us in English! All three were in the Dutch underground. They had been looking for us and knew that six of our crew had been captured by the Germans. Although we were still in hostile territory, we were now linked up with friends.

We walked with them three or four miles to an abandoned house just outside a village. We stayed there until dark. After dark the men returned and took us into the village. We were measured for new clothes, which we were to receive in the next town. Our every move was made in secrecy because there were people who collaborated with the Germans and would have been happy to turn us over to them.

After meeting with the Holland Resistance Army, the four of us were scheduled to move toward Belgium by train. We had been fitted by a tailor with new clothes so we looked Dutch. We were told to follow our leader, a member of the Dutch underground, two at a time. Our instructions were to trail him by about 50 to 75 feet and do exactly as he did.

We were to show no recognition of our leader. Tickets for the train ride had been given to us at the house so it would not be too difficult to follow his example. If caught by the enemy, we would be strictly on our own.

Quite frequently the Germans would move their army equipment on a civilian train. Then if the train was strafed by Allied fighter planes, the Germans would accuse the Allies of shooting at civilians. I hoped the Allies would not pick this train to strafe with their fighter planes.

As we approached the train station, I walked with confidence, even though I was surrounded by German soldiers with their weapons. This "cloak and dagger" walk was easy. The German soldiers did not know we were the enemy because we carried no obvious weapons. I intentionally did not look anyone in the eye; I kept our leader in sight by glancing occasionally in his general direction. The train was filled to capacity, with standing room only. German soldiers with guns were in front, back and both sides of me.

After we stopped at a station, where several passengers got off, I noticed a German soldier look at a vacated seat, then at me. He said something in German. I assumed he was asking if I wanted the empty seat. Not having mastered his language, I thought it best not to answer. Instead I turned away as if I had not heard him, hoping he would do the same and let it pass. He did, and the rest of the train ride went well, though the car was filled shoulder to shoulder with German soldiers.

In August of 1944, the German army was retreating back to Germany during the night. In daylight they hid in a large forest by Rocourt, Belgium. I inspected their bivouac area several times on my way to safety, often from twenty or thirty feet away. The tanks were monstrous and many. Each one was a formidable foe, with drivers, gunners and a skilled and deadly crew. The artillery guns towed by the trucks were huge.

I was not afraid of the Germans because they did not know I was an American. Sometimes the guards would look at me with suspicion, but I was never challenged. Yes, I was at the enemy doorstep, but faith kept me alive. When we allow the Holy Spirit freedom, we find a living faith and courage to spy out the enemy.

Satan's Attack on Jesus

After Jesus fasted in the wilderness for forty days, Satan confronted Him three times with temptation. The apostle Luke writes, "And Jesus, full of the Holy Spirit, returned from the Jordan, and was led by the Spirit for forty days in the wilderness, tempted by the devil" (Luke 4:1–2). Satan's first temptation of Jesus was directed at the Lord's body. Jesus had fasted and in His humanity was hungry. The enemy generally attacks the weak area first, so Satan said to Him, "If you are the Son of God, command this stone to become bread."

Jesus answered him, "It is written, 'Man shall not live by bread alone.'" Satan tried to tempt Jesus in the body but failed.

The enemy did not give up. Satan then took Jesus up to a mountaintop and showed Him all the kingdoms of the world, then said, "To you I will give all this authority and their glory; for it has been delivered to me, and I give it to whom I will. If you, then, will worship me, it shall all be yours."

Jesus answered him, "It is written, 'You shall worship the Lord your God, and him only shall you serve.'"

Then Satan took Jesus to Jerusalem and set Him on the pinnacle of the temple, where he said to Him, "If you are the Son of God, throw yourself down from here; for it is written, 'He will give his angels charge of you, to guard you,' and 'On their hands they will bear you up, lest you strike your foot against a stone.'"

Jesus answered Satan, "It is said, 'You shall not tempt the Lord your God.'" Satan had failed again. (See Luke 4:1–12.)

Three times Jesus used the words "It is written." I know that if Jesus used the Word in spiritual warfare, I, too, need to know the Word for the protection of my spirit, soul and body. I also know that if Christ our Commander recognized Satan, I had better be discerning of the enemy and his tactics.

The apostle Peter tells us, "Be sober, be watchful. Your adversary the devil prowls around like a roaring lion, seeking some one to devour" (1 Peter 5:8). If we do not believe that Satan is a living spirit along with his demon friends, we have been duped and deceived. George Barna, the well-known Christian researcher, found in 2001 that only 27 percent of Americans believe Satan exists. That leaves almost three out of four people wide open to Satan's crippling deceit.

In 1990 I was asked what I would choose if I had a choice of spiritual gifts. I chose discernment. *Discerning* means "to detect or perceive." Discerning in the spiritual realm means that we are able to see into the supernatural and distinguish between the divine Spirit, a human spirit or a demonic spirit. As a soldier of Christ, engaged in spiritual warfare, I need to know what kind of spirits I am encountering. Satan will use whatever method or weapon available to distract, disrupt and destroy our lives. If I cannot discern some of his tactics, I am already a casualty of spiritual warfare.

Shortly after leaving a Bible study one day, I was confronted by a man who asked a question. As he asked the question, my spirit immediately discerned that something was wrong. I asked him a couple of questions to confirm my suspicions, then confronted the demon of lying who had been working through him earlier in the Bible study. Whenever truth had been spoken, he had a different answer, trying to cause disagreement.

I found that this unholy spirit acted similarly to a critical spirit, which is not a spirit of discernment and operates with a tone of superiority. It is generally the human spirit or a demon trying to be God's police officer, speaking in a negative, unloving way. The critical spirit often tries to bend the issue of right and wrong according to its own standards.

The apostle Paul discerned how Satan works, so he writes, "And no wonder, for even Satan disguises himself as an angel of light. So it is not strange if his servants also disguise themselves as servants of righteousness. Their end will correspond to their deeds" (2 Corinthians 11:14–15).

If we are hoodwinked by any of Satan's weapons of warfare, he has power over us. This is why he disguises himself and his cohorts as angels of light. Like chameleons, they blend into the surrounding scene waiting to attack. I have discovered the enemy's main attack weapons are intimidation, temptation, deception, accusation and condemnation.

Intimidation

In February 1997 the enemy tried to overcome me by intimidation. Sitting in my usual chair in the family room, I was suddenly swept into a living hell of extreme vertigo. My mind was spinning as if I was in the vortex of a tornado. While my mind was spinning, my body was quite still. The vertigo was so severe I could barely see beyond the end of my nose.

I immediately knew that demons were trying to frighten and distract me. I had been working on several projects that Satan was not happy about. I had written several articles for the church paper and had many counseling sessions in which people had been set free. The projects and counseling were exposing Satan and his nefarious ways.

Feeling close to losing consciousness, I immediately took authority in Jesus' name and prayed in the Holy

Spirit. I called to Him urgently, expecting to lose my mind or die if He did not intervene. Strange tongues came out of my mouth in force and authority, as the Spirit within me spoke (see 1 Corinthians 12:10). I called on the blood of Jesus for protection.

My wife, sitting close by, noticed my distress and started praying in the Spirit as I was. Speaking in tongues and calling on the blood of Jesus for protection brought an end to the vertigo. As our prayer was answered, I was able to return to normal.

Afterward I asked the Lord why He had allowed the attack. A thought immediately came to my mind: He confirmed that my work was pleasing to Him and hateful to the enemy. I had three other similar attacks, but each time of lesser strength. The battle had been won in spiritual warfare.

Satan's tactics of intimidation depend on fear. Show me people who have never been afraid, and I would say that they have never challenged life. The disciples were afraid after the crucifixion, cowering with fear behind locked doors. Then Jesus appeared on the scene and said, "Peace be with you . . ." (John 20:19).

Fear is a normal consequence of a bold life, but our enemy tries to intimidate us by getting us to look at the circumstance facing us. If that happens, we are not God-centered. Fear given over to God becomes faith.

Temptation

Satan tempts us to break God's laws. Tempting us with immorality, materialism or worldly security, he entices us to make unwise decisions or commit sinful acts.

Satan enjoys leading God's people into temptation. Spiritual warfare was first revealed when the serpent exchanged comments with Eve. Eve was seduced when Satan asked her, "Did God say, 'You shall not eat of any tree of the garden'?" (Genesis 3:1).

The enemy was appealing to Eve's mind, suggesting that what God had said about eating from the Tree of the Knowledge of Good and Evil was not exactly on target. Maybe they misunderstood what God said. Satan was tempting her to doubt God and make an unwise decision. We hear the same type of comment today when people say, "Scripture was written by men." This is the work of Satan, tempting us to question the truth of God's Word.

In the early Christian Church, soon after Pentecost, Ananias and his wife, Sapphira, experienced temptation. They sold their property and wanted to give some of the proceeds to the apostles for distribution. Satan tempted them to pretend that they had given *all* to the apostles, so that people would think better of them.

Peter, discerning that they were holding back, said, "Ananias, why has Satan filled your heart to lie to the Holy Spirit and to keep back part of the proceeds of the land?" (Acts 5:3). Ananias recognized that he had lied to God, fell at Peter's feet and died on the spot.

Peter then confronted Sapphira: "How is it that you have agreed together to tempt the Spirit of the Lord?" (Acts 5:9). Sapphira, hearing the same truth about their sin, fell at Peter's feet and also died.

Ananias and Sapphira fell prey to the temptations of the evil one. There was a crack in their character that was open to temptation. Satan knew exactly where the crack was, so he could enter and tempt them to sin.

If I do not receive what the Lord has for me, I receive what my self-centered old nature working with the enemy has in store for me. My mother used to say, "Life is a two-way street. What you give has a way of coming back to you."

Deception

Jesus exposed the tactics of the enemy when He said, "Simon, Simon, behold, Satan demanded to have you, that he might sift you like wheat, but I have prayed for you that your faith may not fail; and when you have turned again, strengthen your brethren" (Luke 22:31–32).

The Lord warned Peter that Satan was going to use devious tactics to distract him. Jesus knew that Peter would fail during the deception by Satan, but that Peter's faith would rebound when he refocused on Jesus.

Jesus knew that Peter would have several difficult skirmishes with Satan. Perhaps this is why after the resurrection Peter was singled out and blessed when the angel said to the faithful women, "But go, tell his disciples and Peter that he is going before you to Galilee; there you will see him, as he told you" (Mark 16:7).

Peter lost focus several times and failed each time, but in spite of being deceived and knocked down by the enemy, he got up again. The tactic of the enemy was to decieve, but Peter was learning to let God's truth work to overcome the enemy. Peter always got up and looked for Jesus.

Early in our ministry a young married man came to our home. He said, "My wife and I argue about my insincerity and inability to communicate truth. It seems my life is filled with little white lies, which she says make me very unstable. I say one thing and do just the opposite. Can you help me?"

My wife and I listened to him for a little while, and we agreed that he might have a spirit of deception operating in his life. He knelt on the floor and we laid our hands on him, asking the demons their names, then commanding them to come out in the name of Jesus.

We would hear a name of a demon then cast it out by name. Each time, the man gave every indication of a demon leaving by his coughing, spitting and writhing on the floor. This went on for a half-hour. We were getting very tired.

My wife suggested we call Pastor Vaagenes. With reinforcements we laid on hands again with the same results. After fifteen minutes of ministry, the three of us looked up simultaneously at each other. We all discerned that we were dealing with a demon of lying. We cast out the demon of lying and the young man was set free.

The very next morning a vacuum salesman stopped by to demonstrate a vacuum cleaner. In the process, he cleaned the area where the coughing and spitting had occurred. God has a good sense of humor and knows how to encourage us.

The Tolerance Trick

I recently attended a college graduation of about 650 students. There was a spirit of excitement in the room. Fathers, mothers and relatives came together to celebrate this occasion of a loved one passing a certain milestone in life. Many graduates gathered, dressed in the traditional cap and gown, to have their names read and to receive their diploma, a handshake and a sincere "Well done."

Several graduates wore the traditional gown but, in place of the cap, wore lamp shades or wastepaper baskets. They were signaling, in an obvious way, that they had terrible fashion taste.

No, not really. What they were expressing was that they valued their *ability* to express themselves more than they valued tradition—or the feelings and sensibilities of others. Sadly, they probably thought that they were doing a noble thing.

In today's society we hear constantly that we are to be politically correct, which means, in a word, *tolerant.* Society says that we should not take away an individual's right for self-expression, regardless of how outrageous his or her actions might be. It says that we must accept the beliefs, practices and behavior of others—that no one should dictate standards to anyone else.

Although that sounds like good, fair play, it actually makes society a slave to negative people's self-centered acts. We, as Christians, are daily called to become more and more intolerant of society's ugly ideas and attitudes. If we do not call sin (or rudeness!) what it is, we begin to accept it in ourselves.

Satan's deception generally starts out with minor things in life, like the graduation "hats." Then, as his deception takes over a person, he subtly moves to destroy major character values. First it becomes easier to tell white lies, then adultery becomes acceptable; advertising becomes more deceptive, then corporate executives lie to their stockholders.

Satan's deception steals our ability to discern and make wise decisions by trying to make everything acceptable to our minds. We must discern the spirits to see if they are from God. John writes to a Christian community, "Beloved, do not believe every spirit, but test the spirits to see whether they are of God" (1 John 4:1).

Deception Can Be Deadly

Deception is one of Satan's favorite ways to get us off our spiritual course! Many churches have split into two or three groups when invaded by a spirit of deception. The body of believers will be deceived and not be aware of this type of spirit until it has caused disruption, division and permanent damage. A spirit of deception quite frequently takes a pious attitude, seeking to establish itself on center stage and, in a sense, applauds itself on its knowledge and ability to perform. It has its own agenda and will seem to speak sincerely. Often it offers a common Scripture as a Band-Aid fix to a very difficult situation.

At our Sunday evening service there is time for the prophetic voice to be heard. A young man passing through the area attended the service and, believing he had a prophecy, spoke. As he spoke there was utter silence. We could have heard a pin drop. The tone of his voice indicated a spirit of deception. Many of us tested the spirit, discerned it and came to the conclusion that it was not from God.

Jesus spoke of the scribes and Pharisees, "They do all their deeds to be seen by men; for they make their phylacteries broad and their fringes long, and they love the place of honor at feasts and the best seats in the synagogues" (Matthew 23:5–6). The nature of the spirit of deception is pride, using the law as a weapon.

The Deceitfulness of Works

A recent survey of what Christians believe shows that the enemy's deception is frighteningly effective. The survey showed that 39 percent of people who call themselves Christians believe that they can get to heaven by good works. Apparently the truth has been hidden from them.

Paul writes to the Ephesians, "For by grace you have been saved through faith; and this is not your own doing, it is a gift of God—not because of works, lest any man should boast" (Ephesians 2:8–9). If this Scripture is not heart knowledge for us, we will be in bondage, trying by our works to make ourselves acceptable to God. We are acceptable to God because of the shed blood of Jesus Christ and for no other reason. Good works led by the Holy Spirit are simply confirmation of a thriving relationship with Christ.

I was personally deceived for years. I tried to be a better husband, father and friend, but it was by my own striving and conniving. When I understood that entrance into the abundant life was not by my good works but by surrendering to the leading of the Holy Spirit, I found a new freedom!

This survey went on to find that 27 percent of Christians believe that Jesus committed sins. Satan is deceiving about one in four Christians—leading them astray to justify their sins! Their rationalization is that since Christ committed sin, their own sins are no worse. That is deception! The writer to the Hebrews tells us about Jesus, "one who in every respect has been tempted as we are, yet without sin" (Hebrews 4:15).

The survey concluded with the finding that 27 percent of Christians believe that Satan is not a living being. They believe instead that he is a symbol for evil. (Meaning that the interaction between God and Satan in the first two chapters of Job, along with other passages, should be tossed out of the Bible.)

Satan's presence is confirmed in numerous places throughout the Scriptures. The Bible does not say that Jesus was tempted by a symbol of evil in the desert, nor does it say that an "evil symbol" entered Judas. *Satan* found the crack in Judas' heart and deceived him to his own destruction.

Satan appealed to the emotions of Peter when Jesus talked about going to Jerusalem, suffering and dying on the cross. Peter said, "God forbid, Lord! This shall never happen to you." But Jesus turned and said to Peter, "Get behind me, Satan! You are a hindrance to me; for you are not on the side of God, but of men" (Matthew 16:22–23).

Here the spirit of deception used Peter's emotions to make a back-door entrance into his heart and attack the humanity of Jesus.

Satan's work of deception is engineered to bring instability to the Kingdom of God. We need stability as we live in an unstable world—stability that can only come as we depend on and trust God. We become unstable when the enemy deceives us and we are unable to choose God's ways.

John Holum, a retired Augsburg College chemistry professor, once said at a Thursday morning Bible study, "It would be impossible for the world to function if there was not consistency and stability in the elements that make up the chemicals I worked with at the college."

I have seen this principle of stability at work spiritually, in a Bible study group I have attended for more than thirty years. In spiritual warfare, consistency spawns stability.

Those who are consistent in attendance are stable and dependable and have grown the most spiritually.

Stability comes through consistency and obedience to the Lord's leading. As I sought more spiritual stability in my life, the Lord led me one day to Isaiah 33: "The LORD is exalted, for he dwells on high; he will fill Zion with justice and righteousness; and he will be the stability of your times, abundance of salvation, wisdom, and knowledge; the fear of the LORD is his treasure" (verses 5–6).

The work of the Holy Spirit is to teach us healthy spiritual habits. The grace of the Lord will then keep us stable, alert to the enemy's deceptions and alive with faith and expectations. If we stand strong in the fight against intimidation, temptation and deception, the enemy will come as an accuser.

Accusation

In the late 1970s, I was speaking at a charismatic conference in Atlanta, Georgia, on a Saturday evening. Several people who were involved in the service gathered for prayer. As we concluded prayer, a man came and sat on a chair next to me and said, "I have a word from the Lord for you."

I am always eager to hear from the Lord, so I responded, "There are just a few minutes before the service starts. What does the Lord want to tell me?"

He replied, "The Lord said that you have cancer and a root of bitterness."

I thanked him calmly and asked, "Does He have anything else to say?"

He said, "No."

I asked for the man's name and address and told him, "I need your address because you tried to put a curse on me. If you're wrong, you're a false prophet and I need to let you know."

I thanked him calmly again. In my heart I knew this was an attack of Satan, accusing and attempting to divert me from the evening message. The man may not have even known that he was being deceived.

My wife was sitting next to me and heard everything. She was also calm, which I took as a good indication that what he had said was not from God. My wife and I prayed, took authority over the curse and released the Holy Spirit to accomplish what was on His agenda for that evening.

Satan tried to attack me and destroy the evening message through this man. The apostle John writes, "Now the salvation and the power and the kingdom of our God and the authority of his Christ have come, for the accuser of our brethren has been thrown down, who accuses them day and night before our God" (Revelation 12:10).

After the conference I went home and asked Pastor Vaagenes to pray and make sure the curse that had been put on me was broken. Being aware of God's Word, I do not knowingly carry unforgiveness. My spiritual gifts are teaching and encouragement. Unforgiveness would be foreign to and incompatible with these two gifts.

Two months later I wrote to the man suggesting he was prophesying falsely. It was important for him to learn how to discern before he spoke. He had been an instrument of Satan, accusing me when I was not guilty.

Condemnation

The enemy tries using intimidation, temptation, decep-tion, accusation and condemnation to wound us. If he succeeds with any of the first four tactics, he then heaps condemnation upon us. This is a strong feeling of guilt and shame that causes us to hide from God instead of running to Him in repentance.

Condemnation can be self-inflicted or from the enemy. If we are self-centered and introspective, we can be sure that the enemy will give us company to go through our rubbish pile of sins and find condemnation. Satan knows when we have been wounded by one of his four tactics. As we focus on our failures, he stirs our minds with thoughts of hopelessness until we despair and come under con-demnation. This is spiritual warfare!

A young woman came to my wife for help. She and her sister had been molested by a relative. Despite my wife's counsel, the enemy convinced this young lady that she was to blame. Satan kept that thought swirling in her head until it became an obsession. She was so overwhelmed by condemnation that she eventually jumped off a five-story parking ramp, committing suicide. The enemy had been able to convince her that she was unacceptable to society and God.

The apostle John says, "By this we shall know that we are of the truth, and reassure our hearts before him whenever our hearts condemn us; for God is greater than our hearts, and he knows everything" (1 John 3:19–20).

Condemnation is a weapon the accuser uses to hold us in self-imposed bondage. The apostle Paul recognized this and writes, "There is therefore now no condemnation for those who are in Christ Jesus" (Romans 8:1).

There are countless times in life when Satan accuses us of doing something wrong. Sometimes he is right and we have sinned; sometimes he is blatantly lying. Either way, God our Father offers forgiveness and freedom. If we accept Him, there is peace and an end to the accusations. If we accept the condemnation of the enemy, we become helpless and useless.

When the enemy accuses me, I just agree with him that I am a sinner and tell him to take it up with Jesus, who has forgiven me. The enemy backs off because condemnation can never overcome God's redemption.

We need to know the tactics of the enemy—how, when and where he fights. Knowing this, we can then be resilient and spring forward to overcome his intimidation, temptation, deception, accusation and condemnation. We can walk victoriously in spiritual warfare!

9

SATAN'S ARTILLERY BARRAGE

September 8, 1944, five months to the day after I parachuted into enemy-held territory, I was eating breakfast in the home of a widowed member of the Dutch underground. Outside Charles, the son of the widow with whom I was staying, began shouting, "The Americans are here! The Americans are here!"

An American scout patrol had entered the village! I left the breakfast table. I had been waiting five long months for this! When I arrived at the village square, the two American soldiers and their jeep were surrounded by 75–100 people, all trying to hug and kiss them.

These scouts were frontline soldiers of the Allied forces. Their duty was to probe enemy lines for weaknesses and to find secret ways into enemy-held territory. They were to report by radio whenever they saw enemy troops but were not supposed to engage in serious combat. They never knew when they might be ambushed and killed. The scout patrol was a symbol of coming freedom for the people of German-occupied Belgium.

In fact, the American forces were pursuing the German army, which was retreating toward Cologne, Germany. I joined the American soldiers for the day until the commanding officer could arrange my transportation back to Brussels, Belgium, that evening.

About five miles from the village where I had stayed, we came upon a German fortification built into the side of a hill. Several officers, the jeep driver and I went inside to inspect the fortress. As we were inspecting, the ground suddenly shook violently like an earthquake. We raced for the entrance and as soon as we were outside a soldier yelled, "Hit the ground!"

I dove under the jeep for protection from the German artillery. This was my first experience with artillery fire at ground level. The noise and explosions were coming from the deadly 88s, one of Germany's best artillery guns, well-known and respected by the Allies.

Five months earlier I had been shot down by enemy aircraft artillery. As I lay in the dirt, I thought that it would be ironic to be killed by ground artillery just after experiencing freedom.

Satan's Artillery

Artillery is the name we give to large weaponry like cannons, howitzers and missile launchers—weapons that are too heavy to carry. It is an awesome and terrible experience to be on the receiving end of that type of warfare.

The Germans shot at us with their artillery because they wanted to destroy our squad completely. Satan attacks with his best weaponry for the same reason.

When I first experienced the Holy Spirit at my son Rick's funeral, I knew absolutely nothing about spiritual warfare. I did not know that Satan hates all Christians, particularly new ones, and goes into unrelenting battle to get them away from Christ. My first awareness of the enemy came from reading Scripture. I had been told that Satan was not real. But after reading about how Jesus recognized Satan, I decided I had better do the same. I reasoned that unless I was willing to be aware of Satan, I was not ready for a walk of faith—a walk like Jesus'.

I discovered that Satan had my destruction on his mind. As I began to see the evil results of his work in lives and societies that failed to seek God, I decided that I did not want to be one of his victims. Time passed, and I found that there was no middle ground in spiritual warfare—my only choice at any moment was to submit to God or serve the enemy. When I came to this conclusion, I knew that I needed training in spiritual warfare.

Peter writes to the Christians, "Be sober, be watchful. Your adversary the devil prowls around like a roaring lion, seeking some one to devour" (1 Peter 5:8). The example given by the disciples in the New Testament showed me that I should keep everything in perspective. I should be aware of the powers of darkness but not dwell on them. Jesus never said to fear the enemy or to worry about what he would do next. But I understood that this Scripture was my call to be sober and watchful, aware of Satan's intent.

In 1977 the charismatic body of believers in America sponsored an ecumenical conference in Kansas City. The meetings were a beautiful and powerful expression of unity, and the fruits of the conference were so good that the Kansas City committee believed there should also be regional conferences.

Being part of the organizing committee for my region, I set up a meeting with the Catholic music leader to help correlate the worship music. The Catholics sang music that the Lutherans did not and vice versa, so we wanted to strike a good balance. We arranged to meet at a local restaurant.

Upon entering the restaurant, I found myself third in line to be seated. While I waited, I observed a young lady standing off to one side and staring at me.

After just a short time she came over to me and asked, "Are you a businessman?"

I replied, "No, why do you ask?" thinking to myself, *This is a strange encounter!*

She immediately responded, "You seem to have such a peace about you."

As the hostess led me to a booth where I was to wait for my Catholic brother, that comment triggered something within my spirit. I thought to myself, *This is a setup.* Why would this young lady ask such a question? Sure I was peaceful, but why shouldn't I be?

The thought entered my mind: *God is alerting me to spiritual warfare.* As I sat waiting for my friend to appear, it dawned on me that he was not going show up and I would have to eat lunch by myself. I enjoy my own company but this meeting was important. There was not a lot of time to work out the musical differences between Catholics and Lutherans.

I stopped looking toward the restaurant entrance and accepted the fact that he would not appear. The Holy

Spirit had given me notice through the young lady and her question. Rather than being offended or upset, I ordered lunch and had a marvelous time laughing at how God was allowing me to develop patience.

Satan tried to get me angry and upset at my friend for not valuing our meeting. If my self-centered old nature had run things, I would have been unhappy and would not have cared to reschedule the meeting. I would have reasoned that, if my friend did not respect me enough to even show up the first time, why should he care the second time?

In truth, he had simply forgotten and was eager to reschedule. When we finally met we both had a good laugh at God's sense of humor.

Satan thrives on our ignorance in spiritual warfare, but I refused to let the enemy get me upset. If I had gotten upset, I would have been in sin, having lost my focus on God. Sin, intentional or accidental, is Satan's artillery barrage at God!

Satan Targets God

Sin is like a slap in God's face. Satan knows that sin is not only a violation of God's divine law, it is also contrary to the holy character of God. Sin simply cannot exist in God's presence, and it separates us from Him until we confess it and receive His forgiveness. Satan cannot harm God in a direct attack. So he tries to hurt God by separating Him from His children—through our sin.

The Holy Spirit is always working through our consciences, warning us of impending trouble. He is most concerned about our attitudes. If our attitudes are right, the right actions will follow. A negative mind becomes a trap and a place for a satanic artillery barrage.

Years ago I heard someone say, "Learn from other people's mistakes because you will not live long enough to make all of them yourself." We can learn a lot from King David's most infamous mistake—his adultery with Bathsheba.

King David was walking on his rooftop one night when he noticed Bathsheba, a beautiful woman, taking a bath on an adjacent property. David sent a messenger for her and, because he was king, she felt compelled to respond. David then committed adultery with her (see 2 Samuel 11:2–5).

Satan's warfare strategy was to assail David's mind and take away the shock value of sin. This made the adultery seem more acceptable. David knew better, but he let the desires of his self-centered old nature override the consequences of lusting and coveting. David's self-centered old nature tried for a time to justify his actions, but he finally realized he had to take responsibility for his sin.

Under the conviction of the Holy Spirit and his conscience, David said to God, "Against thee, thee only, have I sinned, and done that which is evil in thy sight" (Psalm 51:4). He later went on to say, "Behold, I was brought forth in iniquity, and in sin did my mother conceive me" (Psalm 51:5).

King David knew what was right and he failed to do it. As a result he missed God's will and fellowship. As the apostle James tells us, "Whoever knows what is right to do and fails to do it, for him it is sin" (James 4:17). David discovered that his sin separated him from God. He learned that all sin is against God.

We need to remember not to be judgmental as we look at David's sin. We are not called to be God's police officers.

God has His own way of dealing with the sins of others. Our responsibility is to be aware of our own indiscretions because Satan's artillery is targeting each one of us.

Satan Targets Individuals

God looked at His creation and He pronounced it very good. God does not make failures, but we fail when our attention is diverted from the Creator of life. Satan's basic purpose is to lead us away from the way we were created. The enemy attacks us when we are alone, when we think we are alone and at the times we are least aware of being in danger.

I knew a man who was ambushed this way. While working at his computer, he accidentally clicked on something that brought pornography to the computer screen. It happened more than once and, out of curiosity, he looked a little longer each time.

Next his curiosity led him to deliberately choose pornography pages. The struggle inside him intensified as he violated his conscience "one more time." Finally his conscience could not convict him because he had given it over to the enemy. His superiors found out what he was doing on company time and he lost his job.

Satan Targets Marriages

The Lord taught my wife and me a valuable lesson in spiritual warfare while we were staying in a South Dakota motel. We arrived Saturday afternoon and checked into the motel, hoping to have a time of relaxing before going

167

to dinner. Then we had planned for some evening study on the subject we were to talk about in church—husband and wife relationships.

My wife took her guitar out of its case, sat on a chair and began to sing. After she sang several praise songs, I decided to join in and we both joyfully started to sing the song "In the Name of Jesus."

When we came to the line, "And demons will have to flee," we both heard an audible voice in the room with us. It said, "Lady," in a grumpy, disgusted tone, and then went on to mumble in a harsh, strange sound for about twenty seconds. The voice sounded as though it came from the TV, but the TV was turned off.

My wife and I looked at one another in amazement, wondering what was going on. I opened the door to see if someone had walked by and was offended by our singing, but there was no one in sight.

I immediately went to the motel office and asked, "Is there anyone in rooms six or eight?" (We were in room seven.) He replied, "No, just another couple in room thirteen." I was puzzled. I did not know whether to suspect a demon or write the incident off as a product of our tired imaginations, but I was leaning toward suspecting a demon.

We met with the planning committee at church the next morning before the service. We wanted to seek God's mind so that we would be effective and communicate to the congregation's needs. As we drove home later that day, we rejoiced that the people at church were so loving and warm. We still were concerned by our strange encounter with the voice in our motel room, so I shared the mystery the next morning with veterans in spiritual renewal—Pastor George Voeks and Pastor Rod Lensch.

They agreed, "When you go into a motel room, take authority over the evil spirits. Bind and cast them out in the name of Jesus. Put the room under the blood of Jesus. You do not know what kind of spirits occupied and are still in the room because of the previous lodgers."

Suddenly I understood something about our experiences. Betty and I had traveled to many places, teaching how a Christian husband and wife should function together under God's spiritual principles. We usually had a great time driving to the place where we were to teach. But after we checked into a motel, we often became irritated and would find fault with each other. It is impossible to teach in the Holy Spirit if your spirit is not clean and free from sin, so we would have to work through confession and forgiveness to get our spirits ready to teach.

That day I realized that the demons of deceit had been slyly doing their work over and over again, and we had not even been aware that the enemy was shooting at us. The Holy Spirit taught me two things through that trip to South Dakota:

1. *Take authority over the ungodly spirits in motel rooms.* Clean the room out spiritually and put it under the blood of Jesus.

2. *Walk in authority as a saint.* The apostle Paul writes to the "saints" at Rome, challenging them to the obedience of faith (see Romans 1:1–7). If God calls me a saint, I need a lifestyle of authority that reflects that position.

We are saints who sin but who are saved by grace through the empowering presence of the Holy Spirit. Taking our positions in Christ, we can agree with assurance, confidence and humility that, in spite of being targeted by Satan, we are who God says we are: saints and victors! When Satan shoots at me, I need to discern the attack, raise up my shield of faith and fire back at him with God's Word.

All encounters and situations, natural or supernatural, reveal the will and grace of God. Our part is to pray, discern and act according to God's revelation for that particular situation. Satan will not face God, but he slyly shoots to kill us, our families and friends.

10

FORGIVENESS

Reclaiming Enemy Territory

I remember vividly the tears and shouts of joy as people in the small Belgium village of Rocourt realized that they had been liberated from Nazi occupation. The terrible years of bondage were over! They were free to exercise their wills in a new way and to pursue life as citizens of Belgium once again.

They expressed their joy with celebrations—by dancing in the streets—and by placing wreaths of flowers around the necks of Allied soldiers. Men, women and children alike kissed the soldiers, even throwing their arms around them in profound gratitude.

I did not kiss any of my fellow soldiers, but I was thrilled to see the villagers' expressions of delight because I felt the same way. For me, five months of living within shouting distance of death was coming to a close. I, too, was set free. I could pursue life as an American citizen. I could return to the United States and see what the Air Force had in store for me.

The victory was won in Europe, but we still had an enemy in the great and terrible empire of Japan. There were still battles to be fought, and I knew already that I wanted to be a part. The Army let me ride with them by truck to Paris. Then I flew in a transport plane to England where I was welcomed back by the Eighth Air Force.

Learning Forgiveness

Years later, after the death of my son in Vietnam, I realized the shallowness of my American dream. The big house, airplane and all my other stuff seemed cheap compared to the important things in life. My possessions became worthless in comparison to having a solid spiritual foundation and peace with God. Seeking God became essential to my peace and well-being. New challenges were being brought into my life for my spiritual growth. I began learning the truths of spiritual warfare.

As I began to understand spiritual warfare, I concluded that the enemy liked me to be careless about God's law and my own spiritual discipline. He encouraged me to call sinful laziness and disobedience "depending on grace." The churches I had attended in the past did not call people to spiritual discipline and obedience. The leaders did not confront people who were living sinfully. As a result, there was no declaration of truth to make me aware that I was a sinner. In the absence of law, grace was cheap.

I have found that when grace seems cheap, people come to believe that everyone will get to heaven somehow. Grace without law is cheap because without law there is no sin. Without sin, there is no need for forgiveness. When there is no need for forgiveness, there is no need for a Savior. Without our Lord and Savior Jesus Christ, our faith is empty and powerless. This is a ploy of Satan!

Charles Finney, an evangelist of the eighteenth century, writes, "Misuse of the law is almost certain to result in a false hope; people thinking they are saved when they are not. Failure to use the law introduces a false standard of Christian experience and will fill the Church with false converts."

The Value of Shame and Remorse

If we are going to fight spiritual warfare, we need to know how shame and remorse work. Shame is an emotion of our souls. When we are shamed we feel guilt; we recognize that our actions have made us unacceptable. Remorse is the strength of conviction that makes us willing to humble ourselves and turn 180-degrees away from the shameful act.

God sends shame and remorse to break us free from sin. When we in our self-centered old natures cross the line of discretion, we come under the rule of sin. We need to be set free. Shame and remorse arise to convict us and push us toward forgiveness, restoration and freedom. They fight against sin. That is why I call shame and remorse freedom fighters!

When I was a little boy growing up in northern Minnesota, I sometimes did things that I knew were wrong.

173

Due to my upbringing I had a very healthy conscience. If I stole something or had a fight with a sister, I always felt ashamed about it later. On top of that, I knew that my parents would be disappointed in me if they found out. If my mother caught me in the act, or heard about it later through someone who could not keep a secret, she would say, "Shame on you. You were taught better than that!"

I did not want to hurt my mother, but I seemed powerless against sin. I did not really understand forgiveness, and I certainly did not realize that there was spiritual warfare going on in my soul. So whenever I felt ashamed I just hoped that no one would find out about what I had done. If I could hide my sin long enough, shame would eventually get tired and go away.

After my encounter with God when I was baptized with the Holy Spirit, I discovered that admitting to shame is the first step toward healing. I realized that I feel shame when I have crossed over the line of discretion and violated my conscience. The greater my sin, the greater the shame. The appearance of shame helps me realize that I have made the wrong choice.

Accepted rightly, shame and remorse are like a surgeon's sharp scalpel, cutting to the core of my being, exposing my sin and convicting me to ask for forgiveness. Recognition of shame is the first step to my spiritual recovery. After that I must ask God for forgiveness.

Luke writes, "Repent therefore, and turn again, that your sins may be blotted out, that times of refreshing may come from the presence of the Lord, and that he may send the Christ appointed for you, Jesus" (Acts 3:19–20).

The Necessity of Forgiving Those We Do Not Know . . .

Having accepted God's forgiveness, we are able to forgive those who injure us. The death of my son in Vietnam challenged me to forgive the men who killed him. I knew somehow that if I did not forgive them, I would become bitter, tied forever to his death. It is important for those who survive the death of a loved one in a war to forgive the enemy. I had to make a choice to forgive the ones who killed my son. The alternative to my forgiving was a much higher price. Unforgiveness is like an emotional vampire that sucks out all life.

. . . And Those We Do

A woman made a desperate phone call to my house. With obvious frustration and urgency, she asked, "My husband and I are having a terrible fight and we need help. Would you come right over?"

"Yes, I will be there in about fifteen minutes," I responded immediately. On my way to their home, I prayed for God's wisdom so that I would be sensitive to what was on His heart and how He wanted to resolve their conflict.

As I drove, I thought about the way husbands and wives make their disagreements issues of right or wrong. Each one believes that he is *right*, and so his spouse must be wrong. Neither one really listens to the other; he just waits for his turn to talk again so that he can make his points. The whole time a fight is going on, it is Satan who is winning the battle.

175

I knocked at the door and was confronted by a surly, emotional woman. She asked me in and immediately said, "My husband, in the family room, needs to get his life together. We fight about this issue over and over. I'll never forgive him! I hope you can help him."

I made a mental note that she was holding on to her self-righteousness and expecting her husband to change *his* attitude, and went into the family room, where I was confronted with an angry, frustrated man who was not ready to concede to *anyone*. He said, "I'll never forgive that woman! She always wants to be right." He then motioned me to a chair and I sat down.

The wife entered the room about five minutes after I did. This gave him time to calm down and talk to me about their disagreement. Then she shared a little from her perspective, and he was calm enough to let her talk. Since they were now talking and not arguing, I just listened.

After a short time the Holy Spirit began to break through and get to the crux of their problem. They had been talking about the submission of a wife to her husband. Their conversation had ended up in spiritual warfare because the devil delights in provoking people until emotions get all out of balance.

This couple had not yet discovered that reason and emotions quite frequently fight against one another. When someone is emotional, it is best if the other person does not try to force him to be rational. You cannot argue feelings away, and we cannot rationally discuss *principles* if we are arguing about *feelings*. Whether or not we feel the same emotions, we must give each other permission to have emotional responses—right or wrong! If we do not, there will always be an open door for enemy invasion and unforgiveness.

Sensing their tension subsiding, I asked them to turn their chairs and face one another. Now it was my turn to talk. I said, "Satan has been having a field day. You both need to confess your unforgiveness. Will you face each other, look into your spouse's eyes and ask forgiveness? Then we will pray."

He looked into her eyes and asked for forgiveness. She did the same. He asked God's forgiveness for his part in the dispute. Then she prayed, "Father, forgive me for my bad attitude. Please take my will and make me submissive to my husband!"

After we concluded our prayer I told her, "Though God heard your prayer, there is one part He will not act on. He will not take your will. God's love does not take away our power of choice but challenges us to hear Him, discern truth and exercise our wills.

"You must learn how to exercise your will to make the right choice. If you choose to submit to your husband, God will give you the strength to subdue your selfish nature. But God will not *force* you to submit."

I told them both: "First and foremost, you both need to be submitted to the Holy Spirit. Otherwise your self-centered old natures will make choices for you. Every day is filled with opportunities to forgive, and those who learn that principle will walk in peace and freedom.

"If you are teachable, God will work in your heart first. You force Him to stop when you refuse to forgive. As soon as you forgive, God will go to work on your spouse because you, through forgiving, have been restored."

I told them, "Jesus was denied by Peter, deserted by His disciples, betrayed by Judas and even the Father forsook Him on the cross. But Jesus kept His focus because the nature of our supernatural God is to forgive!"

177

Forgiving from the Heart

I have found that there is a huge difference between forgiving from the head and forgiving from the heart. Many people forgive from the head but still carry the sting from the hurtful incident. I see this expressed when an apology is offered and someone replies, "It's okay."

The truth is, things are not okay. There is hurt involved and we cannot pretend that it is not there. If we do that, the hurt simply sits there, like an open wound. Satan continues to bring the negative incident back to mind, and every bad thing that follows is like salt in the wound because it is a constant reminder of all the hurts we have endured.

Forgiving from the heart does not mean that the incident is forgotten. It means that the Holy Spirit has taken away the hurtful emotion of the incident. A hurt ignored is always valuable to Satan, but a hurt given to God becomes healed. Satan can no longer make an issue out of it. We see a powerful example of forgiveness in the passage where the apostle Stephen was stoned to death. He prayed, "'Lord Jesus, receive my spirit.' And he knelt down and cried with a loud voice, 'Lord, do not hold this sin against them'" (Acts 7:59–60).

When in conflict with someone, I have learned to live by the following truths:

- I ask the Lord to forgive me for my part in the conflict.
- Rather than allow Satan an open door, I forgive the offender whether he deserves forgiveness or not.
- I ask the offended person to forgive me.

178

If I feel led by the Spirit, I pray that the Holy Spirit will bring conviction to the offenders so that they will want to reconcile with me. If they do not come to me, I will confront them after praying and waiting on God's timing. I always try to use a proper tone of voice, not one that is condescending or haughty. I also wait for the right place, being tactful not to confront them before others. Then whether they choose to reconcile or not, I give the incident to the Lord and He helps me to forget about it.

If after all this I feel vindictive, I know that I have not really released the incident to the Lord. Then I have to repent again and ask God to help me to forgive. As long as I hold onto my offended "righteousness" I cannot be right with God. As the psalmist writes, "When I declared not my sin, my body wasted away through my groaning all day long" (Psalm 32:3).

Embellishment, Slander and Bitterness

Unforgiveness is contrary to the Spirit of Christ. When we allow Unforgiveness to live in us, we are without a doubt renting space in our minds to Satan. Worse yet, Unforgiveness has two freeloading cousins that always come to stay: Embellishment and Slander.

Embellishment usually feels invited about the time we are entertaining Unforgiveness with a nice re-hash of the event that hurt us. Since Embellishment is a world-class storyteller, he is always happy to sit down with us and help us remember how badly we were wronged. The sad thing is that Embellishment often adds half-truths, "white lies" and exaggerations—all in the name of poetic license. He especially likes the word *always*, as in: "He *always* says. . . ."

179

Slander does not usually move in until after Embellishment has stayed for a little while. But once Unforgiveness and Embellishment have made a nice cozy nest in your mind, he usually wastes no time in showing up. At that point we cannot help but tell our friends the story of our wrongs. As we justify ourselves and our unforgiveness, Slander uses the lies created by Embellishment to attack the person who has hurt us.

As we indulge our desire to be vindicated, seeking to hurt those who have hurt us, we allow Satan long-term residency in our minds—but not only in our minds. No one can live long with Unforgiveness and avoid becoming bitter. Bitterness grows in the heart, not the mind. It cannot be gotten rid of by mental discipline. It makes us unable to hear the gentle voice of God. Worst of all, it numbs our hearts so that we are unable even to realize that we are bitter. The only hope for a bitter heart is to be overwhelmed by the invasive conviction of the Holy Spirit.

When we become bitter, our enemy has won the battle. We are no longer soldiers in spiritual warfare—we are casualties. Worse than that, we are like soldiers who have been killed by biological warfare; our presence is a danger and a contamination to the believers around us. The author of Hebrews writes, "See to it that no one fail to obtain the grace of God; that no 'root of bitterness' spring up and cause trouble, and by it the many become defiled" (Hebrews 12:15).

Unforgiveness is death. It is death to relationships, death to families, death to churches and death to communities. Forgiveness is life. Taking our place on the cross—crucifying the self-centered old nature—and cutting others some slack brings restoration, freedom and joy. Where the Holy Spirit is, there is freedom that the enemy cannot destroy!

Battlefield Freedom

Betty and I were invited to visit a congregation for several days and talk about relationships and charismatic renewal. When we arrived, we found that teaching on both topics was desperately needed. The church was in turmoil, evenly divided on issues of charismatic truth. Many strong relationships had been hurt or broken. Several families had left the church, and more were threatening to leave.

The pastor and about half of the church council had invited us because they thought that, with some teaching on renewal, relationships could be restored. The rest of the church did not even want us to be there. But considering that, the services were well attended. Our teachings centered on learning how to function in the power of the Holy Spirit and to realize the purpose of the cross. Many people came to the altar for the baptism in the Holy Spirit, but I could sense that there was still unrest among the people.

After the crusade was finished, I asked the pastor and the whole church council to meet with me in a neutral location. We gathered in the back room at a local café. Ten of us sat at a large round table so we could look directly into each other's eyes.

I asked the man to my left to tell us what was on his mind. I said, "There is not to be any rebuttal until everyone has had a turn to speak." As the first man spoke, the tension in the group began to rise. He seemed to be making some serious accusations. As we listened, however, it slowly became clear that he was, in fact, attempting to voice some deep, honestly held concerns.

By the time the third man started to speak, it was obvious that the Holy Spirit was beginning to work. They were being convicted of the hardness of their unforgiving hearts. They had been so busy judging each other that they had forgotten about forgiving one another. As shame and remorse did their work, tears began to flow. There was a breaking down of egos, pride and misunderstanding.

When the last man had finished speaking, I looked around and saw that all of us were crying. The men spontaneously began asking one another for forgiveness and giving it, as confirmed by hugs and (I am sure) the breaking down of satanic walls. I reminded them that when leadership is out of synchronization (with each other or with God), as some of the council members were, Satan has an open door to invade the congregation.

Broken relationships break God's heart, but this church council was being healed through forgiveness. Through genuine forgiveness, the congregation now had a new Spirit-led church council. Now they could do the Father's business. We finished with joyous prayer as we hailed an overcoming victory in Christ.

The Life-Changing Power of Forgiveness

Every now and then our journey through life brings us alongside people who are special. Sometimes we cannot exactly say why they are special, and we do not always know how long they will stay alongside but, in our hearts, we have an immediate and enduring love for them. These special people enhance our lives with their candidness, openness and honesty. They enrich us by being themselves.

Bill was one of those special people in Betty's and my life. Although he was with us only briefly, he made our Christian walk interesting and rewarding. Betty and I held a Monday night Bible study in our home and about 15 to 35 high school and college students generally attended. Bill heard about the Bible study, and he wandered in one Monday night.

He opened up to us right away: "My life has been in shambles with no direction. The Army has drafted me, but I am refusing induction. My family is not happy with my decision and lifestyle. I do not want to be involved in killing. I need some help and direction for my life."

I asked him after the meeting if he had ever given his life to Christ. Bill said, "No, but I am open to whatever helps." We prayed and he became a new Christian. His problems did not go away, but now he had the Holy Spirit to help him in the many decisions he faced.

The following Monday night Bill told us, "The thing that I still have hanging over my head is my refusing induction into the Army. In your Bible study I began to see how God is in control of all things—the government, my parents, my job and my life. I have been rebelling against all of them for a long time."

He went on to say, "I wrestled in my head with my induction this past week. I did not refuse it lightly, and for me to change my mind now seems ridiculous. What will my friends think? What will my family say after I was so adamant against the Army? I need to learn how to bend my will to God's. Will you help me? I am ready to go into the Army if that is where God wants me."

I said, "Bill, you have been extremely teachable. To make a decision like this is commendable! The first item for prayer is asking forgiveness for going your own way. God understands because He looks at your heart [see 1 Samuel 16:7]. Your heart is right. Let's ask God to forgive you for your rebelliousness against your parents, the government and whatever else comes to your mind."

As Bill asked forgiveness, a heavy burden seemed to be taken from him. After our prayer, he was *excited* to go into the Army because he believed that God wanted to teach him something new.

Later, writing to us from the Army, Bill said, "I can truly say that these have been the best years of my life. I have grown closer to the Lord, closer to people and less dependent on the stuff of the world. I am so glad that I learned the truth of forgiveness. The Army gives me lots of opportunity to forgive."

Bill was discharged from the Army and moved to the Carolinas. He married and had a child. One day Bill, his family and a friend went swimming in the Atlantic Ocean. Bill and his friend were caught in a rip tide, a powerful current of water disturbed by an opposing current, and they were swept away from shore. Bill could not handle the pressure of the rip tide and drowned. The undertow was so strong that his friend was barely able to bring Bill's body to shore.

Later Bill's wife wrote to me, "I am so thankful I learned the principles of forgiveness. I know that God allowed my husband's drowning—and I had to forgive God. Through His grace and forgiveness toward me I can pick up the pieces of my shattered life and go on, for I know Bill is in heaven."

Bill's wife learned that whomever you are angry at, even if it is God, it is essential to forgive. She embraced the merit of forgiving in this tragic situation and was set free from the bondage of bitterness. She discovered that forgiveness always brings freedom.

Forgiving Brings Freedom

In the early 1970s I worked with a Christian I did not like. I disliked him because I thought he was self-serving and overbearing, but I knew that unless I dealt with my attitude toward him, I would be a target for Satan and condemnation. As Jesus said, "Make friends quickly with your accuser, while you are going with him to court, lest your accuser hand you over to the judge, and the judge to the guard, and you be put in prison" (Matthew 5:25).

I prayed a lot during that time, and one day it seemed right to approach my co-worker about my attitude. I asked him if I could have some time with him. He agreed. Sitting at a table I said, "I don't like you but we are brothers in Christ. I have a negative attitude toward you, and I need help so that I can change."

He was not aware that I felt resentment toward him and was naturally a little startled. But we talked and I received freedom when I asked him to forgive me for any hurtful things I might have said or done. He also was able to see how some of his actions could appear hurtful to others. The result for both of us was freedom from Satan's trap of disunity.

When we forgive, we disarm Satan and take away his right to be involved. When a cat is declawed, its offensive weapon is taken away. Forgiving declaws the situation and the grace of God allows us to sit in the presence of our former enemy. Forgiveness frees us to be God's ambassadors, bringing His life to a fallen world.

If someone offends you, forgive until it feels good. Let "Will you forgive me?" be your passwords. As we learn to forgive, we reclaim territory that has been conquered by the enemy and bring freedom to ourselves and others.

11

SUFFERING PRODUCES SPIRITUAL MATURITY

There are obvious casualties in any war. Men die. Soldiers carry physical wounds for the rest of their lives: missing limbs, scarred faces and other disfigurations. Where there is warfare there is pain and suffering, and that applies to spiritual warfare as well as physical.

Many times we write off our pain and hardship as part of life. That is true, but it is not the whole truth. Sometimes the pain is a messenger of Satan and can be dealt with accordingly.

Pain and Healing

While attending a conference on the Holy Spirit, I found myself becoming more and more distracted by an extreme pain in my back. Pastor Larry Christenson was the Friday evening speaker. Because Larry always has a fresh spiritual word, I did my best to focus on what he was saying, but it was difficult to concentrate as I squirmed and perspired with the increasing pain.

After the service, I attempted to walk but was unsteady from the intense pain. Betty, noticing my difficulty, assisted me to the car. We were staying along with several other speakers at a local motel. Upon arriving at the motel, I slowly made my way inside and collapsed on the floor, finding it almost impossible to move.

In spite of the excruciating pain, my mind was wondering how Betty and I could conduct a workshop the next morning on speaking in tongues. I could not stand, and I struggled with thoughts of how I would get back to St. Paul and my duties. Could they prop me up somehow? Would I need to travel in a wheelchair, maybe by bus?

Betty went next door and asked Pastors George and Mildred Voeks, speakers at the conference, to lay hands on me and pray for healing. Within minutes they both appeared. I was still on the floor, bound in excruciating pain with my body stiff as a board. George and Mildred laid hands on me and prayed for healing. I knew that God could heal me, but would He?

After praying, George and Mildred left to catch some much-needed sleep, and I remained agonizing on the floor. As I lay there, a Scripture verse came to mind: "Give thanks in all circumstances; for this is the will of God in Christ Jesus for you" (1 Thessalonians 5:18). It was a strange time to think such things, but the verse helped me to refocus from my pain to my Healer.

While still experiencing the terrible pain, I started to say, "Thank You, Jesus! Thank You, Jesus!" Suddenly I felt the presence of Someone in the room with me. I did not see anyone, but I knew that Someone besides my wife had entered the room.

As I continued to give thanks, my toes started to feel hot. The heat began to travel up my legs to my midriff. I continued to give thanks and, with an audible snap, something in my back returned to normal. The pain disappeared immediately, and I jumped up for joy and broke out praising the Lord with several new words in tongues. Does God still miraculously heal today? Ask the man who has been healed!

The next morning, Betty and I had one of the most wonderful workshops we have ever taught. Many participants were baptized in the Holy Spirit and released into a new spiritual language. The presence of the Holy Spirit was at the workshop just as He was in my room the night before. This struggle was clearly the result of spiritual warfare!

God has healed me several times, and I have learned that I need to go to Him first. If I am not healed miraculously, I then claim His Scripture promises and go to the doctor.

Righteous and Unrighteous Suffering

I know that all pain and healing is in God's hands. As John writes, "No one can receive anything except what is given him from heaven" (John 3:27). Many times our suffering is a tool in the loving hand of God, like Paul's thorn in the flesh. Pain can be God's way of alerting us that something needs to change. It can be a wake-up call so that we stop taking life for granted and begin to take stock of what we are doing and why.

If, for example, a rotten tooth did not ache, we might wait too long to get treatment and end up having the tooth pulled rather than simply filled. Pain and suffering are good if they are allowed to accomplish their purposes. Scripture reveals that there are two kinds of suffering.

1. Suffering from Unrighteousness

If we plant evil in the soil of life, we will harvest hurt. It is as simple as cause and effect, but it is deeper than that. Paul explains this spiritual principle to the Galatians: "Do not be deceived; God is not mocked, for whatever a man sows, that he will also reap. For he who sows to his own flesh will from the flesh reap corruption; but he who sows to the Spirit will from the Spirit reap eternal life" (Galatians 6:7–8).

I remember lying on the sandy ground, a nine-year-old boy too sick to get up, but writhing in pain from stomach convulsions. It seemed to me that I was dying and life would soon be over. I began to think that maybe I should not have overindulged in a big candy bar. Who knew (besides the mother I had disobeyed) that it would make me so sick? I knew better than to eat the whole thing, but that candy tasted so good while I was eating it!

As a skinny little boy I could not help myself out of the dilemma that I had brought on myself. I needed help. The only one who could help me was fifty to sixty feet away. Not wanting to cry, because males are "not supposed to cry," but sobbing with all my might, I summoned what little strength I could muster and weakly called out, "Mom, I'm sick."

Mothers are generally intuitive and perceptive concerning their children. My mom just happened to go by a window at that moment. Glancing out, she saw that this miserably sick child of hers was in deep trouble.

Running out the doorway, she quickly scooped up my weak, sick body in her arms. As she tenderly carried me toward the house, she assured me that I would be okay. Shame and remorse were already doing their duty of convicting me, and I had determined before we got inside that I would not overindulge again.

My suffering was the result of my actions, and I saw clearly that I was reaping what I had sowed! On a small scale, I had learned to identify unrighteous suffering.

2. Suffering for Righteousness' Sake

This pain comes when we suffer because we are Christians. When we stand up for Christ, we become an obstacle to those who want to live without Him. Our attitudes and lifestyles should be different from that of worldly people who do not know Christ. This may make non-Christians resentful, which means we will suffer because of their attitudes. We who chose to follow Christ will be excluded, ridiculed and scoffed at because of our Christian persuasion.

Ananias, a disciple of Jesus Christ, received a message from God concerning Saul who was renamed the apostle Paul. Luke recorded God's words: "I will show him how much he must suffer for the sake of my name" (Acts 9:16).

Many Christians live in hostile lands. Hundreds are martyred every year for their Christian faith. We in America have not come to the point of shedding our blood, but we suffer heartache over millions of aborted babies, the decline of morality, the spurning of the Christ and the preaching of a different gospel. The apostle Peter writes: "For one is approved if, mindful of God, he endures pain while suffering unjustly" (1 Peter 2:19). That is righteous suffering.

A friend named Mike described what happened to him when he turned to God after a horrible experience in his life. He said, "None of my family would accept me after I came to know God. My siblings turned their backs on me. My mother had died, but my father joined my sisters and brothers in rejecting me.

"I suffered the absence of their understanding and companionship. They did not invite me to the usual family gatherings. We used to go out as a group for dinner and have lots of laughter, but that became a thing of the past. It hurt me deep inside."

He went on to say, "What Satan meant for evil God used for good! As long as my family rejected me, I sought after God with a new intensity in my heart. God brought new friends into my life, people who shared my desire for Him.

"While studying God's Word one day, I came upon a verse that applied to my situation. The apostle Paul wrote to the Romans, 'If possible, so far as it depends upon you, live peacefully with all' [Romans 12:18]. I decided that the Holy Spirit was challenging me to test this principle with my family. I saw that I needed to meet them where they were at. I stopped talking about Christ and began to listen to them.

"As they talked, the barriers between us began to be broken down. The Lord was depending on me to be sensitive to their needs. As our relationships were restored, I gradually began to tell them what was happening in my life.

"My siblings and father were now more open to hear me. In the fullness of God's time, my oldest sister asked why I had changed so much for the good. She said, 'I have always loved you as my brother. You are so much easier to be around today than in the past.'"

Mike was learning about suffering as he stood up for God.

Nine of God's Uses for Suffering

Suffering in life does not go away, but I have discovered that learning some of the basic reasons for suffering makes the affliction more bearable.

1. Pain and Suffering Are Wake-up Calls

Pain and suffering lead us to evaluate and take stock of our attitudes toward God and life. Are we taking life for granted? Are our lives without meaning? Paul tells us, "Examine yourself, to see whether you are holding to your faith. Test yourselves. Do you not realize that Jesus Christ is in you?—unless indeed you fail to meet the test!" (2 Corinthians 13:5).

What if a telephone call comes from the doctor as we are getting the children ready for school? What if he has noticed a dark spot on the X-ray he took recently? Our initial thought is: *Is it cancer?* Or, if the spot is on the heart: *Will I have a heart attack?*

Both questions can produce an extremely uneasy feeling, because *cancer* and *heart attack* are words that make us face death. Satan feeds our thoughts with speculation and conjecture, creating a fear of the unknown. Unless

193

we allow the Holy Spirit to guard the perimeters around our mind, anxiety becomes overwhelming!

Questions flood our minds: *Why me? Where is God in this? Will He walk through this with me? Is there a purpose in this?* Worry and anxiety take our minds off Christ. But if we can put our minds back on Him, this situation can give rise to much healthier questions: *What kind of mark will my life leave on eternity? Have I done the truly important things today? Am I secure in God's plan for me and my family?* This is spiritual warfare!

To know Christ intimately requires understanding and accepting the purpose of pain and suffering. When there are no struggles, we do not seem to grow spiritually. It is in pain and suffering that we seek and search and are drawn closer to God.

2. Suffering Can Bring Us Closer to God

In 1990 Betty and I received news from California that our 36-year-old son had committed suicide. Our son could not reconcile himself to his brother's death in Vietnam. He, too, was a casualty of Vietnam.

The pain that hit our hearts was overwhelming. We were staggered but not knocked down. Betty and I believe in God's sovereignty. God did not cause our son's suicide, but He allowed it to happen. Through our suffering we drew closer to God to seek an answer.

Suicide reflects a hopeless society where many people have lost all purpose. Despair steals hope, and that is why we should never deprive someone of hope. It might be the only bit of God they have left to hang onto. A Christian brother who had heard of our son's suicide asked, "What about my brother who also committed suicide? Will he be in heaven? Is he a casualty of spiritual warfare?"

I replied, "We are not called by God to decide who has salvation. That decision lies only in God's hands. A suicide should spur us who know the love of Christ to take that love to those who are on the verge of losing hope. When hope is gone, the mind says, 'There is no reason to live.' God always gives hope and assurance to the survivors of a suicide."

I told him, "I know that some people believe it is not possible for those who commit suicide to go to heaven. I believe that God's grace is bigger than our often-narrow understanding of His Word."

Jesus indicated to Pilate that the power over life belongs to God and no one else. Jesus said, "You would have no power over me unless it had been given to you from above" (John 19:11).

The author of Job writes, "In his hand is the life of every living thing and the breath of all mankind" (Job 12:10).

Solomon repeats what many Scriptures say: "No man has power to retain the spirit, or authority over the day of death" (Ecclesiastes 8:8).

God has provided the entrance to heaven based on Jesus' suffering and dying for us on the cross. John explains this salvation succinctly when he writes: "But to all who received him, who believed in his name, he gave power to become children of God" (John 1:12). But what does that belief look like? Is it a particular theology? Is it an intellectual understanding at the time of death?

I say no, because that would immediately eliminate special-education children, those with Alzheimer's disease and countless others who do not have the mental capacity to comprehend reality. I believe that this group includes those who have lost hope and commit suicide. They are so despairing and unaware that they stand at the portal of eternity!

We need to remember that Jesus also said to the unbaptized criminal on the cross, "Truly, I say to you, today you will be with me in Paradise" (Luke 23:43). This is a good sign that God has the final word in life-and-death situations, even at times to destroy man's theology. The following poem sums it up:

> I dreamt the other night, heaven's gates swung open
> wide,
> A kindly angel ushered me inside.
> Indignant words rose to my lips, but never were set
> free.
> Stunned surprise showed on every face,
> Not one expected me!
>
> Anonymous

The psalmist tells of God's sovereignty:

> Thou knowest when I sit down and when I rise up; thou discernest my thoughts from afar. Thou searchest out my path and my lying down, and art acquainted with all my ways. Even before a word is on my tongue, lo, O LORD, thou knowest it altogether.
>
> Psalm 139:2–4

This Scripture, along with many others, tells us that God knows a person's every thought. That includes the thought patterns that lead to despair and sometimes suicide. It is a time of grieving, because this mystery touches the lives of all who knew the person. If we know someone who has committed suicide, it should be a time for reflecting, not for being judgmental. We need to ask why the church did not intervene as this person suffered an emotional breakdown, loneliness and despair.

When we face suffering, the work of the Holy Spirit is completed only when we are conformed to the image of Christ. Many Christians go through tough trials but learn nothing that would bring them closer to being obedient to their call from God.

3. Suffering Calls Us to Obedience

For years I was under the illusion that God allowed suffering in my life to help me become holy as He was holy. I would try harder to be a good and holy Christian. I suffered much as I struggled on in the strength of my sinful, self-centered old nature. Finally I came to understand that holiness is a by-product of God's testing. My main call is not to holiness, but to *obedience.*

So often in life we confuse the goal with the strategy to get to the goal.

The author of Hebrews says, "Although he was a Son, he learned obedience through what he suffered" (Hebrews 5:8). If Christ suffered in His humanity, can we, His people, expect anything less? That is the reason for the cross, that we might become like Him in His death. It takes obedience to achieve the goal!

4. Suffering Brings Insight

My wife answered the doorbell one evening and was confronted by a weeping wife and a huffy husband. My wife, sensing their distress, encouraged him to go into our family room where I was reading. She stayed in the living room to talk with his wife.

He burst into the family room with an aggressive attitude. "My wife has a problem!"

I immediately responded, "I am sure it is you. If a wife has a problem, so has the husband." We started to talk, and he quickly admitted that his wife had discovered that he had committed adultery.

My wife was able to calm his wife down after a while, and they came into the family room. It was obvious that her heart was filled with pain. As we talked, he began to break down from his surly attitude and share how he got involved in adultery.

He said that his wife was too busy with their three children, who were between 18 and 23 years old. He and his wife did not communicate well at home because her mind always seemed to be on her children's welfare. She was occupied with legitimate concerns, but they left him outside the circle.

He lived his life under the same roof as his wife, but there was no intimacy. He honestly felt that he had tried to interact with her, but she was always busy. Finally he began to set up a life that excluded an intimate relationship with her. Soon he met a woman at work who happened to relate on a level he was looking for. The inevitable happened. They committed adultery.

There was no excusing the husband's sinful behavior. It was wrong and brought them both pain and emotional suffering. But God used the suffering to bring a revelation of truth.

As the husband confessed, his wife received the insight that she had made herself too busy. In spite of the pain and suffering he had caused her, she was willing to start reconciliation. They faced each other, looked into each other's eyes and asked forgiveness. God had used pain to bring insight, and when they reconciled and decided to work at their marriage, Satan lost that battle of spiritual warfare.

Suffering brought Job spiritual insight. He lost not only his family but his health as well. God used the suffering to show Job how weak his own righteousness was and gave him insight into the majesty and mercy of God. As little children we hear, "Boys don't cry." A comment comes our way: "Take it like a man." Our early stages of growth are filled with admonitions to stand on our own two feet. I am sure that Job had a struggle giving up his righteousness for God's.

But as soon as Job humbled himself and accepted the revelation God had for him, the Lord restored him and doubled what he had lost before the enemy's attack. Job said, "I had heard of thee by the hearing of the ear, but now my eye sees thee; therefore I despise myself, and repent in dust and ashes" (Job 42:5–6).

5. Suffering Reveals Our Attitudes

Suffering brings us face to face with who we are and our mortality. Peter puts it succinctly: "Beloved, do not be surprised at the fiery ordeal which comes upon you to prove you, as though something strange were happening to you" (1 Peter 4:12).

The Serenity Prayer gives good advice: "God grant me the serenity to accept the things I cannot change; courage to change the things I can; and wisdom to know the difference" (Reinhold Niebuhr). The only thing about suffering that I can change is my attitude. I cannot even change my wife's attitude! Nor can she change mine.

I have had a healthy physical life, and when I made hospital calls it was difficult to empathize with the sick. I did not understand the struggle to choose a God-honoring attitude. God helped me by taking me through back trouble so severe that I could hardly walk. The excruciating pain and physical suffering brought me a new attitude toward suffering. They say that there are no atheists in foxholes. Well, there are even fewer hypocrites in pain! Suffering will show you what kinds of selfishness you secretly carry around. Then you can give them over to God.

6. Suffering Produces Endurance

I was on the track team in high school and began my training as a sprinter. But in competition, after running several sprints, I often entered a race of several miles.

I generally would lead the races starting out, but after a bit I began to falter because I had not trained for the long race. My mind gave up before my body did, and I consistently lost the longer races. Only after a few weeks of refocusing and training for endurance was I able to complete the longer races.

Suffering, discernment, obedience, understanding and endurance generally come in that order. As we suffer, meaningless things are stripped away. We become more focused, appreciative of the gift of life and willing to endure to the end. Paul writes to the Romans, "More than that, we rejoice in our sufferings, knowing that suffering produces endurance, and endurance produces character, and character produces hope" (Romans 5:3–4). Spiritual character might be described as valuing the things God values. A person with godly character becomes one of a kind with God.

7. Suffering Produces Fellowship

I called on a man who was dying from cancer in a hospital. He lived in a small town, out of state. The last time he had been in church, five years earlier, he had a disagreement with the church council. He felt they had done him wrong and vowed never to go to church again.

He was reluctant to talk, but as I challenged him the Holy Spirit began to break through the barriers he had erected against the church. As I led him in a prayer of forgiveness his eyes began to glisten, and then the tears started to flow like a flood. He was releasing the pent-up emotions that had been buried for years. His wife and I joined in, and the three of us cried because of the forgiveness and relief he experienced.

The fellowship of the Holy Spirit was expressed through tears, laughter and joy. We shared in his brokenness and obvious relief from bearing a burden that he was not supposed to carry. His confessing, forgiving and cleansing were part of spiritual warfare!

Many times pain and suffering can make us vulnerable, which helps to bring a deeper dimension to our relationships. I meet with a large group of believers who share each other's pain as caregivers and friends—not only intellectually but emotionally. As we struggle together, we begin to experience in a small way the suffering our Lord went through on the cross. In His fellowship we receive comfort in our suffering. We then are called to comfort others with the comfort we received.

John writes, "That which we have seen and heard we proclaim also to you, so that you may have fellowship with us; and our fellowship is with the Father and with his Son Jesus Christ" (1 John 1:3).

8. Suffering Establishes Us in the Faith

To be established is to allow our spirits of adventure to cross the line of discretion and develop into strong faith. The suffering I have gone through has established me in a stronger relationship with God. As the apostle Paul writes, "Through whom we have received grace and apostleship to bring about the obedience of faith . . ." (Romans 1:5). Despite a falling stock market and the threat of terrorism, I believe God still has everything under His control. I do not know what the future holds, but I know He holds the future in His hands.

Years ago a friend, Linda Morken, was diagnosed with multiple sclerosis, a disease that debilitates, disables and eventually kills those who suffer with it. Linda, a young mother, was lying on a sofa too sick to move. Matthew, her three-year-old son, came in from play and wanted some chocolate chip cookies. There were none because Linda had been too sick to bake cookies.

Matthew went to his mom, laid hands on her and prayed, "God, heal my mom so she can get up and make me chocolate chip cookies." He then went back outside to play. Suddenly, Linda experienced something happening in her body!

In spite of excruciating pain, she slowly raised to a sitting position. With great difficulty she was able to get off the sofa. The closer she got to the kitchen, the easier each step became. As she prepared the ingredients for the cookies, she began to feel much better. The Holy Spirit working through the faith of a three-year-old was sufficient to heal her of multiple sclerosis! She has walked in her healing for more than thirty years.

9. Suffering Brings Comfort to Others

In the early 1990s, my wife started to show signs of memory loss. Several years later other symptoms began to indicate the possibility of Alzheimer's disease. Since then she has been diagnosed with that disease and is in a nursing home.

A friend asked me how I feel after visiting her. I replied, "Each time I leave my heart is broken, and something within me dies. As I look into her blue eyes I know that the girl I married is not there."

Her body is there, but her brilliant mind is not the same. The mind is like a keyboard on a computer. At times we touch certain keys and get results different from what we want. The screen is there, but we do not receive what we need. Likewise, hidden somewhere within her body is my beautiful wife, but I do not know what key to press to bring her back.

The apostle Paul writes to the Corinthians,

Blessed be the God and Father of our Lord Jesus Christ, the Father of mercies and God of all comfort, who comforts us in all our affliction, so that we may be able to comfort those who are in any affliction, with the comfort with which we ourselves are comforted by God.

2 Corinthians 1:3–4

I have joined a caregivers' group that meets at the nursing home once a month. About fifteen to twenty people come together to share a common concern—how to function without a spouse. As we share, we comfort, encourage and support one another. We learn to live with suffering by sharing our suffering!

Why not allow our pain and suffering to be a catalyst, helping others to be drawn closer to God? This can be accomplished when we learn through pain and suffering to allow the Holy Spirit to make us mature soldiers.

Everyone suffers in some way, but how we handle suffering is important. Many people take an "I am a victim" mentality. For some that is a place to start, but if we stop there we miss God's benefits.

I have discovered that how I relate to pain and suffering determines whether I walk in victory or defeat in spiritual warfare. I decided against the stoic approach of hiding the pain and suffering inside, never passing beyond that point. To know Christ intimately requires understanding and accepting the purpose of pain and suffering. When there are no struggles, we do not grow spiritually. It is in pain and suffering that we are challenged to stop relying on ourselves and draw closer to God.

Good suffering is when we learn from the pain. As we grow in understanding, we become aware of our part in pain and suffering. When it strikes, we immediately appeal to God and ask Him to turn it into a positive experience.

The apostle Paul summarizes the purpose of suffering: "That I may know him and the power of his resurrection, and may share his sufferings, becoming like him in his death" (Philippians 3:10). Our call is to make sure it is good suffering, because suffering is part of life and spiritual warfare!

12

MINISTERING ON
THE BATTLEFIELD

World War II ended with the dropping of two atomic bombs on the mainland of Japan and the Japanese empire's subsequent surrender. But hundreds of loyal Japanese soldiers refused to believe that the surrender was genuine. Because they would not admit defeat, pockets of fierce fighting continued for some time after the war had officially ended. Many American soldiers lost their lives during this crucial but largely ignored phase called "mopping up."

I have discovered that my part in spiritual warfare is the mopping-up operation. Christ won the victory on the cross. My call is to proclaim that victory to those who are in bondage to the world. As a vessel for the Holy Spirit,

I am to overcome my local pockets of resistance to the Gospel and help others to experience God on earth.

The church I attend today had about six hundred members in 1970, with only a few attending regularly. Many of the people were members in name only, occasionally attending on Christmas and Easter or for a wedding or a funeral. It was typical of churches at that time. Today the church has two campuses with more than eight thousand members, nine worship services, 130 active ministries, a kindergarten-through-eighth-grade academy and a host of other ministries. The mature ministry of this body has touched many lives around the world.

This change came about because of the ministry of Pastor Morris Vaagenes, who came to the church in the mid-1960s. Pastor Morris had been brought up in the denominational church, but he was not locked into traditionalism. He wanted the members of his congregation to know Jesus personally and to follow the Holy Spirit.

As Pastor Morris reflected on his early ministry, the Holy Spirit showed him that he spent most of his time patching up problems. Instead of pouring truth into people who wanted to know Jesus, he was babysitting troublemakers and discontented grumblers.

Pastor Vaagenes sensed that Bible studies could help him meet the needs of hungry believers. He started a few, focusing on teachings about the spiritual gifts and God's desire for us to become mature in faith. As the hungry saints discovered and were released in their spiritual gifts, God began to reveal His heart and dreams for the church. The ministry grew—not only spiritually, but numerically— as they began applying God's truth to their lives.

In the past denominational churches have grown from within. Large families automatically had their newborn babies baptized; young people married and brought their spouses into the church. That was how the church grew in number. This is no longer true. Today families are smaller, more transient and less apt to be involved in the church. They will not park themselves in one place and remain there simply because it is proper or traditional.

Pastor Larry Christenson, author and international speaker, said in a workshop at an International Lutheran Conference on the Holy Spirit: "Tradition is the living faith of the dead. Traditionalism is the dead faith of the living!"

Traditions that are born of the Holy Spirit will continue to express the will and desire of God. We are challenged to hold them fast because they are foundational to life and spiritual growth. Spirit-filled traditions are stepping stones from the past to the present and future. Paul tells the Thessalonians: "So then, brethren, stand firm and hold to the traditions which you were taught by us, either by word of mouth or by letter" (2 Thessalonians 2:15).

The growth of any church today is correlated with a willingness to be dependent on the Holy Spirit, be teachable and be open to the Holy Spirit's moving (see 1 Corinthians 12:4–11). The presence of spiritual warfare in every congregation confirms our need for the gifts of the Spirit. Paul writes to the Corinthians: "Now concerning spiritual gifts, brethren, I do not want you to be uninformed" (1 Corinthians 12:1).

I found that the gifts of the Spirit are cultivating tools that God uses to produce the fruit of the Spirit in His people. Spiritual fruit does not just appear. A tree must be nurtured, watered and pruned before it will bear fruit. The same truth holds true for Christians. The gifts and fruit of the Holy Spirit work together in order that people can experience God's love through us. That is why a Spirit-filled Christian is a dangerous challenge to Satan.

Under the encouragement of Pastor Vaagenes, the men and women of our church began to take leadership roles. They laid hands on the sick, at home and in the hospitals, and prayed for healing. They implemented a ministry that reached several nursing homes. Lay speakers were invited to visit other churches. Our "ministry staff" became a priesthood of believers in action.

The Priesthood of Believers

One of the most profound and ever-challenging spiritual truths revealed to Martin Luther was the "priesthood of believers." God intended that the body of believers would learn how to minister to one another. To *minister* means "to serve one another, to give of our assistance and attention." This means that all members of the Body of Christ are ministers who represent God's Kingdom here on earth!

To help everyone be a minister, God has given five spiritual gifts. Paul names these gifts in Ephesians: "And his gifts were that some should be apostles, some prophets, some evangelists, some pastors and teachers" (Ephesians 4:11).

Paul then writes the job description for the gifts mentioned above: "To equip the saints for the work of ministry, for building up the body of Christ" (Ephesians 4:12). The people who fall into these five categories of spiritual leadership are responsible for training all other believers to do the work of ministry. The Great Commission is to go and make disciples of all nations. A church without disciples has a pastor who is not fulfilling his call. Anything less than preparing the laity to minister is playing church!

I believe that one of the most difficult trials a church can go through is breaking the traditional mentality that laity cannot do anything spiritual. "We pay our pastor to do the ministry" is the attitude of many traditionalists. But the apostle Peter writes to Christians everywhere: "You are a chosen race, a royal priesthood, a holy nation, God's own people, that you may declare the wonderful deeds of him who called you out of darkness into his marvelous light" (1 Peter 2:9).

God told Jeremiah, "For my people have committed two evils: they have forsaken me, the fountain of living waters, and hewed out cisterns for themselves, broken cisterns, that can hold no water" (Jeremiah 2:13). I believe that the modern-day denominational church has forsaken the "fountain of living waters," which is the Holy Spirit. In His place we have hewed out committee by-laws and ministry programs. God yearns for all of His people to be mature and available for ministry!

As ministers before God, we need first to be aware of His indwelling Spirit. We must be willing, sensitive and dependent on the Holy Spirit to guide us in everything we do.

The Five Areas of Ministry

We need to prioritize our ministry into five areas: ministry to God, ministry to ourselves, ministry to spouses and family, ministry to the priesthood of believers and ministry in the marketplace of life.

1. *If I minister to God first, the priorities of my day will fall into their right places.* The writer of Chronicles tells

209

us that God desires His people to minister to Him: "Aaron was set apart to consecrate the most holy things, that he and his sons for ever should burn incense before the LORD, and minister to him and pronounce blessings in his name for ever" (1 Chronicles 23:13).

I read years ago that God desires for us to praise Him, and I said to God, *You must have a bigger ego than I do. Why am I to praise You?*

A thought immediately came to my mind: *I do not need your praise. You need to praise Me because praise takes your focus off your problems. As you praise Me, you will discover Me as the solution to your problems!*

I have discovered that there are numerous ways to minister to God. We minister first through recognition of Him, then through praise, obedience and the many ways in which we acknowledge that He comes first in our lives.

One of the ways I minister to God is to greet Him with a positive attitude first thing in the morning. Nothing should keep me from recognizing Him when I awaken to morning consciousness. After saying good morning, I also spend time in Bible-reading and prayer, unless circumstances make it impossible.

Another way to minister to God is to sing to Him. The psalmist says to God: "Yet thou art holy, enthroned on the praises of Israel" (Psalm 22:3). As we sing, our focus changes and we see things as they really are. Our problems and the enemy's attacks are subject to the Lord, who sits enthroned over everything He has created.

Our lifestyles minister to the Lord when we are consciously aware of Him, teachable and willing to be different from worldly people. As we seek to bless God, He will reveal to us the many ways in which He desires to interact with His children. We can minister to Him simply by desiring to know Him and to bless Him.

2. *When we minister to God, we will also be ministering to ourselves.* Jesus said, "You, therefore, must be perfect, as your heavenly Father is perfect" (Matthew 5:48). Peter reiterated, "But as he who called you is holy, be holy yourselves in all your conduct" (1 Peter 1:15).

Of course we know that it is impossible for our flesh to be perfect or holy. Jesus, being the only perfect one, calls us to exchange our lives for His. This can happen only when we surrender our lives to Him on a daily basis. As we step aside from our self-centered old natures, He lives His life through us, just as water passes through a pipe. The result is that we are built up, encouraged and ministered to.

Solomon gives a word of wisdom in Proverbs: "My son, be attentive to my words; incline your ear to my sayings. Let them not escape from your sight; keep them within your heart. For they are life to him who finds them, and healing to all his flesh" (Proverbs 4:20–22).

I used to struggle with God's admonishment to love my neighbor as myself. How could I be that unselfish? It was when I realized that I *could not* truly love my neighbor that I was able to relax and let Christ do the job. My call was submission to the Holy Spirit who loves my neighbors through me.

When we minister to other people, we are sharing the truth and love that God has given to us. We cannot give away what we do not have any more than we can return from where we have not been. If we do not spend time with God, we minister out of a dull, starved and insensitive spirit that has not been energized by the Holy Spirit!

211

3. *Our spouses and families should be our third ministry priority*—right after blessing God and being ourselves filled with the Spirit. If a husband and wife take time to minister and bring out the best in each other, their whole family will prosper.

Paul writes to the Ephesians: "Husbands, love your wives, as Christ loved the church and gave himself up for her" (Ephesians 5:25). What wife would not love her husband if he loved her as Christ loved the Church? When a husband loves his wife, their children feel safe and secure. Children respond to positive leadership in the home by being respectful, and they will grow spiritually as well as physically.

Peter speaks to the wives: "But let it [your beauty] be the hidden person of the heart with the imperishable jewel of a gentle and quiet spirit, which in God's sight is very precious" (1 Peter 3:4). Physical beauty passes with age, but the inward spirit is what makes a woman beautiful.

If we seem spiritual at church but do not have a healthy family ministry, we are hypocrites. If we are not fun to live with, we need to examine our priorities and the spiritual influences we allow into our lives. Satan is always close by, waiting like a roaring lion to pounce upon our spouses and families. By not having a conscious awareness of the Holy Spirit, we give Satan an open door to attack and destroy our family. I believe that this is why there are so many divorces in Christian families.

Betty wanted to start family devotions when the children were young, but I did not really support her at the time. Now, years later, I believe that my family and I could have avoided many pitfalls had I been rooted and grounded in Jesus Christ. Daily prayer and devotions could have been a foundation stone in a richer, fuller life.

4. *The fourth group we minister to is the priesthood of believers.* Paul writes, "So then, as we have opportunity, let us do good to all men, and especially to those who are of the household of faith" (Galatians 6:10).

According to 1 Corinthians 14:3, the ingredients of prophecy are upbuilding, encouragement and consolation. I believe that these three things should be a part of all body ministry. People often have difficulty seeing God's hand at work in their own situations. We must seek to discern the work of God in each other and then speak truth and encouragement.

But do not be too quick to offer a solution. Speaking too quickly can prevent us from discerning the prompting of the Holy Spirit. Solomon said, "If one gives answer before he hears, it is his folly and shame" (Proverbs 18:13). If we answer before we listen, we might offer a Band-Aid to cure a heart condition.

This is why operating in the spiritual gifts can be so important to our ministries. The world has nothing to offer. We have nothing to offer. Only Jesus has the words of life. We need to help each other focus on Him, because that is the greatest ministry of all.

5. *The fifth place to minister is the marketplace of life.* Paul tells the Corinthians, "All this is from God, who through Christ reconciled us to himself and gave us the ministry of reconciliation" (2 Corinthians 5:18).

If we have the first four aspects of ministry in their proper place, the Holy Spirit will give us audience in the world. There is no need for us to strive to "reach the lost." If our prayer is for the Holy Spirit to lead and guide us, then everyone we meet is an opportunity to present Christ. Our lives are the New Testament that people in the world will read!

Bold Witness for the Lord

Not everyone is called to be an evangelist, but everyone is called to be a *witness*—"to furnish evidence or
testify of what we have seen or heard." All of the members of our church have been challenged to witness for
God. Some witness for the Lord by working at shelters,
visiting people in prison or by serving in other ways.
Their lifestyles show their concern for people who do
not know Christ.

I believe in lifestyle evangelism. It means that through
our lifestyles others will be led by the Holy Spirit to ask,
"What makes you different? I know life has not been easy
for you, but you seem to rise above the circumstances.
How and why?" But to the man who had been set free
from demons, Jesus said, "Go home to your friends, and
tell them how much the Lord has done for you, and how
he has had mercy upon you" (Mark 5:19). I believe that
God wants to incorporate both a silent and a spoken
witness into our lives. We should be servants who are
eager to tell the good news of Christ.

I remember getting on an elevator with Betty and Jon
Mostrom. The elevator was on the sixth floor of a building
in downtown Minneapolis and already crowded before
we got in. I was last on the elevator, so my back was to
the elevator door. I looked at the six strangers staring
back at me, and spontaneously said, "I suppose you are
all wondering why I called this meeting."

A harsh voice immediately spoke up from the back:
"What are you selling?"

Smiling at them I replied, "Jesus Christ. Not too long
ago the spaceship Challenger exploded and seven souls
went into eternity. Where will yours go?"

There was complete silence until we reached the first floor. As I backed out of the elevator I heard a man say, "I wish I hadn't asked."

I felt sorry for the man who made the comment because his response showed me his hardness toward God. I forgave him for the comment and prayed that God would work in his heart. Because of my witness, the Holy Spirit now had ammunition with which to convict him.

Witnessing is easy if we are focused on God. When we are led by the Holy Spirit witnessing becomes an adventure because He provides the opportunities. Our part is simply to discern the Holy Spirit's leading. I usually give a witness about Christ soon after I meet a stranger.

We need Holy Spirit power to witness. Our call to maturity and spiritual warfare is only one side of the coin; the other side is a call to witness. Witnessing is a powerful spiritual weapon against the enemy. Other people may disagree with your interpretation of the Scripture, but it is difficult to discount someone else's experience.

I have discovered there are five foundational reasons for giving my witness.

1. *According to the Bible, God expects us to witness.* As a rule, the Christian community has done a lot less witnessing ever since Satan began spreading the lie that faith is supposed to be personal and private. We need to believe again that our message is good news and meant to be shared!

I learned that I needed to admit, deep in my heart, that God can (and does) choose to use me. There is no room in spiritual warfare for false humility. If the Holy Spirit had wanted someone else to do my "job," He would have asked him!

Moses says in Exodus, "Oh, my Lord, I am not eloquent, either heretofore or since thou hast spoken to thy servant; but I am slow of speech and of tongue" (Exodus 4:10). Moses was trying to wiggle out of God's calling by saying that he was incapable—that he was a poor public speaker. After pointing out that He had *made* Moses' tongue, God told Moses that He was not interested in his capability, but in his availability!

Jesus said the same thing in the New Testament: "You did not choose me, but I chose you and appointed you that you should go and bear fruit and that your fruit should abide" (John 15:16).

2. *I need to be reminded of how God rescued me from eternal death.* This is, most importantly, a reminder of His love and a call for me to be thankful. It is also a challenge; out of my thankfulness and love grows a desire to have a pure heart.

A pure heart, like ministry, is a fruit of my relationship with God. They must go together so that I do not dump my own issues and problems into the lives I minister to. If I am not right with God, I will minister only half-truths, leaving room for the enemy's deceit. I must make sure that my conscience is clear, as Paul writes to Timothy: "The aim of our charge is love that issues from a pure heart and a good conscience and sincere faith" (1 Timothy 1:5).

3. *I need to be reminded of how the Holy Spirit continually renews me, so that I will not take Him for granted.* I did not grow spiritually until I began to share my testimony with others. Witnessing comes naturally out of an active, living relationship with God. When I speak of what God means to me, He affirms what I mean to Him by renewing my mind and answering prayer. By interacting with me, He affirms that we are walking together.

4. *Satan needs to be reminded of whom I now belong to.* When the enemy attacks my thoughts, I witness out loud to how the Holy Spirit is working in my life. Satan always disappears because he hates to hear how he is losing the battle.

5. *Others need to hear how I have been saved and am living in the victory of spiritual warfare.* The apostle Paul writes, "I planted, Apollos watered, but God gave the growth" (1 Corinthians 3:6). Just as Paul planted seeds, we, too, must be seed planters. Our call is not to lead everyone to Christ but to be witnesses of Him within our spheres of influence.

The harvest time belongs to the Holy Spirit. Only He knows the human heart and when someone is ready to say yes to Christ. After a seed has been planted, it needs Holy Spirit watering to germinate. If we try to pluck an apple off a tree before it is ready, it resists and quite frequently tastes terrible because it is not ripe. Likewise, trying to badger people into receiving Christ before the Holy Spirit has prepared them for that step is precipitous.

Jesus said, "My food is to do the will of him who sent me, and to accomplish his work. Do you not say, 'There are yet four months, then comes the harvest'? I tell you, lift up your eyes, and see how the fields are already white for harvest" (John 4:34–35).

As I travel through life, I have discovered that there is always an alternative to God's way. It is not a path of joy. It is a more costly choice. I have counted the cost and have come to the conclusion that God's way is best!

The priesthood of believers needs to train God's recruits in ministry and spiritual warfare. It is our time in history to step forward in complete abandonment to God and be all that we can be!

AFTERWORD

PEACE AT LAST

Sailing into Boston Harbor in 1944 brought a lump to my throat and tears to my eyes. At last I was seeing again the mighty country for which I, along with many millions of others, had been willing to sacrifice. In the course of that sacrifice I had discovered that I loved her more than I had known.

Even today, as I look at the flag and remember the many who did not come home—who gave their lives for the freedom our flag symbolizes—my heart is warmed and my tears often flow freely.

Franklin Roosevelt said, "Those who have long enjoyed such privileges as we enjoy forget in time that men and women have died to win them." It is sad how many Americans presume upon the freedom that has been given to us by those who died.

Arnold Toynbee, a British historian and educator, said, "Twenty-three out of twenty-five civilizations have died from apathy within two hundred years." We, as a nation, are more than two hundred years old and showing great signs of moral apathy and decay. I believe that, in the future, we will succumb to apathy and anarchy unless we turn to God. As Solomon says, "Righteousness exalts a nation, but sin is a reproach to any people" (Proverbs 14:34).

I conducted polls on several occasions, asking church-goers: "If you died today, where would you go?" Some people answered, "Heaven, I hope." Some said they would go "wherever my friends are." Some said they were Lutheran, as if there is a special place in the universe for departed Lutherans! In sum, most of the people I polled did not know what would happen to them after they died.

Like me, many Christians have been swindled out of their assurance of eternal life. The apostle John tells it as it is: "And this is the testimony, that God gave us eternal life, and this life is in his Son. He who has the Son has eternal life; he who has not the Son of God has not life" (1 John 5:11–12). If we do not even have certainty in our salvation, we cannot venture very far in a relationship with God!

Keeping us from that relationship is the work of Satan, and as long as we have an enemy to contend with, spiritual warfare will never be ended on earth. Will you join me—you who are God's chosen people—and walk in the victory Christ has won for us through the cross? If we desire the fulfillment of our Christian destinies, we have no choice but to engage in spiritual warfare!

Jesus challenges us: "The Spirit and the Bride say, 'Come.' And let him who hears say, 'Come.' And let him who is thirsty come, let him who desires take the water of life without price" (Revelation 22:17).

Dick Denny is a native of Minnesota who had a life-changing experience when his firstborn son died in Vietnam in 1968. Faced with his son's death, Dick was challenged to find what life is truly about. He had achieved the American dream but found that his achievements could not help him deal with the loss of his son.

Called by the Holy Spirit in 1970, he became involved in the charismatic renewal that the Spirit was pouring out at that time. Dick served as a business manager for Lutheran Youth Encounter (LYE), as a pastoral lay assistant, as an executive secretary for Lutheran Charismatic Renewal Service and as the national coordinator for the International Renewal Center in St. Paul, Minnesota. During his time with the Center, Dick was manager of the International Lutheran Conference on the Holy Spirit in Minneapolis, which drew 25,000 Spirit-filled Christians from around the world.

Dick has spoken at hundreds of churches and conferences, both in America and overseas. Today he spends his time writing, teaching and counseling. His heart's desire is to see God's people come into their full inheritance in Christ.